CROCK·POT

· THE ORIGINAL SLOW COOKER ·

SLOW COOKER RECIPES

Publications International, Ltd.

Table of Contents

Slow Cooking Tips

Sizes of CROCK-POT®
Slow Cookers

Smaller **CROCK-POT®** slow cookers—such as 1- to 3½-quart models—are the perfect size for cooking for singles, a couple or empty nesters (and also for serving dips).

While medium-size **CROCK-POT®** slow cookers (those holding somewhere between 3 quarts and 5 quarts) will easily cook enough food at a time to feed a small family, they are also convenient for holiday side dishes or appetizers.

Large **CROCK-POT®** slow cookers are great for large family dinners, holiday entertaining and potluck suppers. A 6- to 7-quart model is ideal if you like to make meals in advance, or have dinner tonight and store leftovers for another day.

Types of CROCK-POT®
Slow Cookers

Current **CROCK-POT®** slow cookers come equipped with many different features and benefits, from auto cook programs to oven-safe stoneware to timed programming. Please visit

WWW.CROCK-POT.COM to find the **CROCK-POT®** slow cooker that best suits your needs.

How you plan to use a **CROCK-POT®** slow cooker may affect the model you choose to purchase. For everyday cooking, choose a size large enough to serve your family. If you plan to use the **CROCK-POT®** slow cooker primarily for entertaining, choose one of the larger sizes. Basic **CROCK-POT®** slow cookers can hold as little as 16 ounces or as much as 7 quarts. The smallest sizes are great for keeping dips warm on a buffet, while the larger sizes can more readily fit large quantities of food and larger roasts.

Cooking, Stirring and
Food Safety

CROCK-POT® slow cookers are safe to leave unattended. The outer heating base may get hot as it cooks, but it should not pose a fire hazard. The heating element in the heating base functions at a low wattage and is safe for your countertops.

Your **CROCK-POT®** slow cooker should be filled about one-half to three-fourths full for most recipes unless otherwise instructed. Lean meats such as chicken or pork tenderloin will cook faster than meats with more connective tissue and fat such as beef chuck or pork shoulder. Bone-in meats will take longer than boneless cuts. Typical **CROCK-POT®** slow cooker dishes take approximately 7 to 8 hours to reach the simmer point on LOW and about 3 to 4 hours on HIGH. Once the vegetables and meat start to simmer and braise, their flavors will fully blend and meat will become fall-off-the-bone tender.

According to the U.S. Department of Agriculture, all bacteria are killed at a temperature of 165°F. It's important to follow the recommended cooking times and not to open the lid often, especially early in the cooking process when heat is building up inside the unit. If you need to open the lid to check on your food or are adding additional ingredients, remember to allow additional cooking time if necessary to ensure food is cooked through and tender.

Large **CROCK-POT®** slow cookers, the 6- to 7-quart sizes, may benefit from a quick stir halfway through cook time to help distribute heat and promote even cooking. It's usually unnecessary to stir at all, as even ½ cup liquid will help to distribute heat and the stoneware is the perfect medium for holding food at an even temperature throughout the cooking process.

Oven-Safe Stoneware

All **CROCK-POT®** slow cooker removable stoneware inserts may (without their lids) be used safely in ovens at up to 400°F. In addition, all **CROCK-POT®** slow cookers are microwavable without their lids. If you own another slow cooker brand, please refer to your owner's manual for specific stoneware cooking medium tolerances.

Frozen Food

Frozen food can be successfully cooked in a **CROCK-POT®** slow cooker. However, it will require longer cooking time than the same recipe made with fresh food. It's almost always preferable to thaw frozen food prior to placing it in the **CROCK-POT®** slow cooker. Using an instant-read thermometer is recommended to ensure meat is fully cooked through.

Pasta and Rice

If you are converting a recipe for a **CROCK-POT®** slow cooker that calls for uncooked pasta, first cook the pasta on the stovetop just until slightly tender. Then add the pasta to the **CROCK-POT®** slow cooker. If you are converting a recipe for the

CROCK-POT® slow cooker that calls for cooked rice, stir in raw rice with the other recipe ingredients plus ¼ cup extra liquid per ¼ cup of raw rice.

Beans

Beans must be softened completely before combining with sugar and/or acidic foods in the **CROCK-POT®** slow cooker. Sugar and acid have a hardening effect on beans and will prevent softening. Fully cooked canned beans may be used as a substitute for dried beans.

Vegetables

Root vegetables often cook more slowly than meat. Cut vegetables accordingly to cook at the same rate as meat—large or small or lean versus marbled—and place near the sides or bottom of the stoneware to facilitate cooking.

Herbs

Fresh herbs add flavor and color when added at the end of the cooking cycle; if added at the beginning, many fresh herbs' flavor will dissipate over long cook times. Ground and/or dried herbs and spices work well in slow cooking and may be added at the beginning of cook time. For dishes with shorter cook times, hearty fresh herbs such as rosemary and thyme hold up well. The flavor power of all herbs and spices can vary greatly depending on their particular strength and shelf life. Use chili powders and garlic powder sparingly, as these can sometimes intensify over the long cook times. Always taste the finished dish and correct seasonings including salt and pepper.

Liquids

It's not necessary to use more than ½ to 1 cup liquid in most instances since juices in meats and vegetables are retained more in slow cooking than in conventional cooking. Excess liquid can be cooked down and concentrated after slow cooking on the stovetop or by removing meat and vegetables from stoneware, stirring in one of the following thickeners and setting the **CROCK-POT®** slow cooker to HIGH. Cover; cook on HIGH for approximately 15 minutes or until juices are thickened.

Flour: All-purpose flour is often used to thicken soups or stews. Stir cold water into the flour in a small bowl until smooth. With the **CROCK-POT®** slow cooker on HIGH, whisk the flour mixture into the liquid in the **CROCK-POT®** slow cooker. Cover; cook on HIGH 15 minutes or until the mixture is thickened.

Cornstarch: Cornstarch gives sauces a clear, shiny appearance; it's used most often for sweet dessert sauces and stir-fry sauces. Stir cold water into the cornstarch in a small bowl until the cornstarch dissolves. Quickly stir this mixture into the liquid in the **CROCK-POT®** slow cooker; the sauce will thicken as soon as the liquid simmers. Cornstarch breaks down with too much heat, so never add it at the beginning of the slow cooking process and turn off the heat as soon as the sauce thickens.

Tapioca: Tapioca is a starchy substance extracted from the root of the cassava plant. Its greatest advantage is that it withstands long cooking, making it an ideal choice for slow cooking. Add it at the beginning of cooking and you'll get a clear, thickened sauce in the finished dish. Dishes using tapioca as a thickener are best cooked on the LOW setting; tapioca may become stringy when boiled for a long time.

Milk

Milk, cream and sour cream break down during extended cooking. When possible, add them during the last 15 to 30 minutes of slow cooking, until just heated through. Condensed soups may be substituted for milk and may cook for extended times.

Fish

Fish is delicate and should be stirred into the **CROCK-POT®** slow cooker gently during the last 15 to 30 minutes of cooking time. Cover; cook just until cooked through and serve immediately.

Baked Goods

If you wish to prepare bread, cakes or pudding cakes in a **CROCK-POT®** slow cooker, you may want to purchase a covered, vented metal cake pan accessory for your **CROCK-POT®** slow cooker. You can also use any straight-sided soufflé dish or deep cake pan that will fit into the stoneware of your unit. Baked goods can be prepared directly in the stoneware; however, they can be a little difficult to remove from the insert, so follow the recipe directions carefully.

Colcannon (page 162)

Appetizers

Easiest Three-Cheese Fondue

MAKES 8 SERVINGS

2 cups (8 ounces) shredded
Cheddar cheese
¾ cup milk
½ cup crumbled blue cheese
1 package (3 ounces) cream
cheese, cut into cubes
¼ cup finely chopped onion

1 tablespoon all-purpose flour
1 tablespoon butter
2 cloves garlic, minced
4 to 6 drops hot pepper sauce
⅛ teaspoon ground red pepper
Breadsticks and assorted
cut-up fresh vegetables

1. Combine Cheddar cheese, milk, blue cheese, cream cheese, onion, flour, butter, garlic, hot pepper sauce and ground red pepper in **CROCK-POT®** slow cooker. Cover; cook on LOW 2 to 2½ hours, stirring halfway through cooking time.

2. Turn **CROCK-POT®** slow cooker to HIGH. Cover; cook on HIGH 1 to 1½ hours or until heated through. Serve with breadsticks and vegetables.

Warm Blue Crab Bruschetta

MAKES 16 SERVINGS

4 cups peeled, seeded and
diced plum tomatoes

1 cup diced white onion

⅓ cup olive oil

2 tablespoons sugar

2 tablespoons balsamic vinegar

2 teaspoons minced garlic

½ teaspoon dried oregano

1 pound lump blue crabmeat,
picked over for shells

1½ teaspoons kosher salt

½ teaspoon cracked black
pepper

⅓ cup minced fresh basil

2 baguettes, sliced and toasted

1. Combine tomatoes, onion, oil, sugar, vinegar, garlic and oregano in **CROCK-POT**® slow cooker; stir to blend. Cover; cook on LOW 2 hours.

2. Stir crabmeat, salt and pepper into **CROCK-POT**® slow cooker, taking care not to break up crabmeat. Cover; cook on LOW 1 hour. Fold in basil. Serve on baguette slices.

SERVING SUGGESTION: Crab topping can also be served on Melba toast or whole grain crackers.

Asian Barbecue Skewers

MAKES 4 TO 6 SERVINGS

2 pounds boneless, skinless chicken thighs

½ cup soy sauce

⅓ cup packed brown sugar

2 tablespoons sesame oil

3 cloves garlic, minced

½ cup thinly sliced green onions (optional)

1 tablespoon toasted sesame seeds (optional)*

To toast sesame seeds, spread in small skillet. Shake skillet over medium-low heat 2 minutes or until seeds begin to pop and turn golden brown.

1. Cut each chicken thigh into four pieces, about 1½ inches thick. Thread chicken onto 7-inch-long wooden skewers, folding thinner pieces, if necessary. Place skewers into **CROCK-POT**® slow cooker, layering as flat as possible.

2. Combine soy sauce, brown sugar, oil and garlic in small bowl. Reserve ⅓ cup sauce; set aside. Pour remaining sauce over skewers. Cover; cook on LOW 2 hours. Turn skewers over. Cover; cook on LOW 1 hour.

3. Remove skewers to serving platter. Discard cooking liquid. Pour reserved sauce over skewers. Sprinkle with green onions and sesame seeds, if desired.

Sausage and Swiss Chard Stuffed Mushrooms

MAKES 6 TO 8 SERVINGS

4 tablespoons olive oil, divided
½ pound bulk pork sausage
½ onion, finely chopped
2 cups chopped Swiss chard
¼ teaspoon dried thyme
2 tablespoons garlic-and-herb-flavored dry bread crumbs
1½ cups chicken broth, divided
½ teaspoon salt, divided

½ teaspoon black pepper, divided
2 packages (6 ounces *each*) cremini mushrooms, stemmed*
2 tablespoons grated Parmesan cheese
2 tablespoons chopped fresh Italian parsley

Do not substitute white button mushrooms.

1. Coat inside of **CROCK-POT**® slow cooker with nonstick cooking spray. Heat 1 tablespoon oil in medium skillet over medium heat. Add sausage; cook and stir 6 to 8 minutes or until browned. Remove sausage to medium bowl using slotted spoon.

2. Add onion to skillet; cook and stir 3 minutes or until translucent, scraping up any browned bits from bottom of skillet. Stir in chard and thyme; cook 1 to 2 minutes or until chard is wilted. Remove from heat.

3. Stir in sausage, bread crumbs, 1 tablespoon broth, ¼ teaspoon salt and ¼ teaspoon pepper. Brush remaining 3 tablespoons oil over mushrooms. Season with remaining ¼ teaspoon salt and ¼ teaspoon pepper. Fill mushrooms evenly with stuffing.

4. Pour remaining broth into **CROCK-POT**® slow cooker. Arrange stuffed mushrooms in bottom. Cover; cook on HIGH 3 hours. To serve, remove mushrooms using slotted spoon; discard cooking liquid. Combine cheese and parsley in small bowl; sprinkle evenly over mushrooms.

Party Mix

MAKES 10 CUPS

3 cups rice squares cereal
2 cups toasted oat ring cereal
2 cups wheat squares cereal
1 cup pistachio nuts or peanuts
1 cup thin pretzel sticks
½ cup (1 stick) butter, melted

1 tablespoon Worcestershire sauce
1 teaspoon seasoned salt
½ teaspoon garlic powder
⅛ teaspoon ground red pepper (optional)

1. Combine cereals, nuts and pretzels in **CROCK-POT**® slow cooker.

2. Mix butter, Worcestershire sauce, seasoned salt, garlic powder and ground red pepper, if desired, in small bowl. Pour over cereal mixture in **CROCK-POT**® slow cooker; toss lightly to coat.

3. Cover; cook on LOW 3 hours, stirring well every 30 minutes. Cook, uncovered, on LOW 30 minutes. Store in airtight container.

Spiced Beer Fondue

MAKES 1½ CUPS

2 tablespoons butter

2 tablespoons all-purpose flour

1 can (8 ounces) light-colored beer, such as ale or lager

½ cup half-and-half

1 cup (4 ounces) shredded smoked gouda cheese

2 teaspoons coarse grain mustard

1 teaspoon Worcestershire sauce

⅛ teaspoon salt

⅛ teaspoon ground red pepper

Dash ground nutmeg (optional)

Apple slices and cooked potato wedges

1. Melt butter in medium saucepan over medium heat. Sprinkle with flour; whisk until smooth. Stir in beer and half-and-half; bring to a boil. Cook and stir 2 minutes. Stir in cheese, mustard, Worcestershire sauce, salt and ground red pepper; cook and stir until cheese is melted.

2. Coat inside of **CROCK-POT**® "No Dial" slow cooker with nonstick cooking spray. Fill with warm fondue. Sprinkle with nutmeg, if desired, and serve with apples and potatoes.

Thai Coconut Chicken Meatballs

MAKES 4 TO 5 SERVINGS

1 pound ground chicken
2 green onions, chopped
1 clove garlic, minced
2 teaspoons toasted sesame oil
2 teaspoons mirin
1 teaspoon fish sauce
½ cup unsweetened canned coconut milk

¼ cup chicken broth
2 teaspoons packed brown sugar
1 teaspoon Thai red curry paste
1 tablespoon canola oil
2 teaspoons lime juice
2 tablespoons water
1 tablespoon cornstarch

1. Combine chicken, green onions, garlic, sesame oil, mirin and fish sauce in large bowl. Shape into 1½-inch meatballs. Combine coconut milk, broth, brown sugar and curry paste in small bowl; stir to blend.

2. Heat canola oil in large skillet over medium-high heat. Working in batches, brown meatballs on all sides. Remove to **CROCK-POT®** slow cooker. Add coconut milk mixture. Cover; cook on HIGH 3½ to 4 hours. Stir in lime juice.

3. Stir water into cornstarch in small bowl until smooth; whisk into sauce in **CROCK-POT®** slow cooker. Cook, uncovered, on HIGH 10 to 15 minutes or until sauce is slightly thickened.

TIP: Meatballs that are of equal size will be done at the same time. To ensure your meatballs are the same size, pat seasoned ground meat into an even rectangle and then slice into even rows and columns. Roll each portion into a smooth ball.

Juicy Reuben Sliders

MAKES 24 SLIDERS

1 corned beef brisket (about 1½ pounds), trimmed
2 cups sauerkraut, drained
½ cup beef broth
1 small onion, sliced
1 clove garlic, minced

4 to 6 whole white peppercorns
¼ teaspoon caraway seeds
48 slices pumpernickel or cocktail rye bread
12 slices deli Swiss cheese
Dijon mustard (optional)

1. Place corned beef in **CROCK-POT**® slow cooker. Add sauerkraut, broth, onion, garlic, peppercorns and caraway seeds. Cover; cook on LOW 7 to 9 hours.

2. Remove corned beef to large cutting board. Cut across grain into 16 slices. Cut each slice into 3 pieces. Place 2 pieces corned beef on each of 24 slices of bread. Place 1 heaping tablespoon sauerkraut on each sandwich. Cut each slice of Swiss cheese into quarters; place 2 quarters on each sandwich. Spread remaining 24 slices of bread with mustard, if desired, and place on top of sandwiches.

Soy-Braised Chicken Wings

MAKES 2 DOZEN WINGS

¼ cup dry sherry

¼ cup soy sauce

3 tablespoons sugar

2 tablespoons cornstarch

2 tablespoons minced garlic, divided

2 teaspoons red pepper flakes

2½ pounds chicken wings, tips removed and split at joints

2 tablespoons vegetable oil

3 green onions, cut into 1-inch pieces

¼ cup chicken broth

1 teaspoon sesame oil

1 tablespoon sesame seeds, toasted*

To toast sesame seeds, spread in small skillet. Shake skillet over medium-low heat 2 minutes or until seeds begin to pop and turn golden brown.

1. Combine sherry, soy sauce, sugar, cornstarch, 1 tablespoon garlic and red pepper flakes in large bowl; stir to blend. Reserve ¼ cup marinade in separate small bowl. Stir wings into remaining marinade. Cover; marinate in refrigerator overnight.

2. Drain wings; discard marinade. Heat vegetable oil in large skillet over high heat. Add wings in batches; cook 3 to 4 minutes or until browned on all sides. Remove to **CROCK-POT**® slow cooker using slotted spoon.

3. Add remaining 1 tablespoon garlic and green onions to skillet; cook and stir 30 seconds. Stir in broth; pour over wings. Cover; cook on HIGH 2 hours.

4. Remove wings to large serving platter using slotted spoon. Add sesame oil to reserved marinade; stir to blend. Pour over wings; sprinkle with sesame seeds.

Beef and Lettuce Wraps

MAKES 8 APPETIZER SERVINGS

1 pound ground beef

1 medium red bell pepper, chopped

1 cup water

1 can (12 ounces) water chestnuts, chopped

1 small onion, chopped

2 cloves garlic, minced

2 tablespoons soy sauce

2 tablespoons seasoned rice vinegar

2 tablespoons chopped fresh cilantro

1 or 2 heads leaf lettuce, separated into leaves (discard outer leaves)

Hoisin sauce (optional)

1. Brown beef in large skillet over medium-high heat 6 to 8 minutes, stirring to break up meat. Drain fat. Remove to **CROCK-POT**® slow cooker. Add bell pepper, water, water chestnuts, onion, garlic, soy sauce and vinegar. Cover; cook on HIGH 3 hours or until vegetables are tender. Turn off heat. Stir in cilantro.

2. Spoon beef mixture onto lettuce leaves; sprinkle with hoisin sauce, if desired. Wrap lettuce leaves around beef mixture to make wraps.

Bacon-Wrapped Scallops

MAKES 12 SERVINGS

24 sea scallops, side muscle removed
½ cup Belgian white ale
3 tablespoons chopped fresh cilantro

2 tablespoons honey
¼ teaspoon chipotle chili powder
12 slices bacon, halved

1. Pour ½ inch of water in bottom of **CROCK-POT**® slow cooker. Combine scallops, ale, cilantro, honey and chipotle chili powder in medium bowl; stir to coat. Refrigerate 30 minutes.

2. Place 1 scallop on end of 1 bacon half. Roll up jelly-roll style and secure with toothpick. Remove to large baking sheet. Repeat with remaining bacon and scallops. Brush tops of scallops with ale mixture.

3. Heat large skillet over medium heat. Add wrapped scallops; cook 5 to 7 minutes or until bacon is just beginning to brown. Remove to **CROCK-POT**® slow cooker. Cover; cook on LOW 1 hour.

Pork Tenderloin Sliders

MAKES 12 SANDWICHES

2 teaspoons chili powder
¾ teaspoon ground cumin
½ teaspoon salt
½ teaspoon black pepper
2 tablespoons olive oil, divided
2 pork tenderloins (about 1 pound *each*)
2 cups chicken broth

12 green onions, ends trimmed
½ cup mayonnaise
1 canned chipotle pepper in adobo sauce, minced
2 teaspoons lime juice
12 dinner rolls, sliced in half horizontally
12 slices Monterey Jack cheese

1. Coat inside of **CROCK-POT**® slow cooker with nonstick cooking spray. Combine chili powder, cumin, salt and black pepper in small bowl. Rub 1 tablespoon oil evenly over each pork tenderloin. Sprinkle cumin mixture evenly over tenderloins, turning to coat. Heat large skillet over medium heat. Cook tenderloins 7 to 10 minutes or until browned on all sides. Remove to **CROCK-POT**® slow cooker; add broth and green onions. Cover; cook on LOW 6 to 8 hours.

2. Combine mayonnaise, chipotle pepper and lime juice in small bowl; stir to blend. Cover and refrigerate.

3. Remove pork and green onions to large cutting board. Coarsely chop green onions. Thinly slice pork. Evenly spread chipotle mayonnaise on bottom halves of rolls. Top with green onions, tenderloin slices and cheese. Replace roll tops. Serve immediately.

Fiesta Dip

MAKES 16 SERVINGS

8 ounces canned refried beans

½ cup (2 ounces) shredded Cheddar cheese, plus additional for garnish

⅓ cup chopped green chile pepper*

¼ cup salsa

Tortilla or corn chips

Chopped fresh tomatoes

*Chile peppers can sting and irritate the skin, so wear rubber gloves when handling peppers and do not touch your eyes.

Combine beans, ½ cup cheese, chile pepper and salsa in **CROCK-POT®** "No Dial" slow cooker. Cover; cook 45 minutes or until cheese is melted, stirring occasionally. Serve on tortilla chips. Garnish with tomatoes and additional cheese.

Red Pepper Relish

MAKES 8 SERVINGS

4 large red bell peppers, cut into thin strips

2 small Vidalia or other sweet onions, thinly sliced

6 tablespoons cider vinegar

¼ cup packed brown sugar

2 tablespoons vegetable oil

2 tablespoons honey

½ teaspoon salt

½ teaspoon dried thyme

½ teaspoon red pepper flakes

½ teaspoon black pepper

2 baguettes, sliced and toasted

Combine bell peppers, onions, cider vinegar, brown sugar, oil, honey, salt, thyme, red pepper flakes and black pepper in **CROCK-POT**® slow cooker; stir to blend. Cover; cook on LOW 4 hours. Serve on baguette slices.

Pork Meatballs in Garlicky Almond Sauce

MAKES 6 SERVINGS

½ cup blanched whole almonds
1 cup chicken broth
⅓ cup roasted red pepper
4 teaspoons minced garlic, divided
1 teaspoon salt, divided
½ teaspoon saffron threads (optional)

1 cup fresh bread crumbs, divided
¼ cup dry white wine or chicken broth
1 pound ground pork
¼ cup finely chopped onion
1 egg, lightly beaten
3 tablespoons minced fresh Italian parsley

1. Place almonds in food processor; process until finely ground. Add broth, red pepper, 2 teaspoons garlic, ½ teaspoon salt and saffron, if desired; process until smooth. Stir in ¼ cup bread crumbs. Remove to **CROCK-POT**® slow cooker.

2. Place remaining ¾ cup bread crumbs in large bowl; sprinkle with wine and stir gently. Add pork, onion, egg, parsley, remaining 2 teaspoons garlic and ½ teaspoon salt; mix well. Shape pork mixture into 24 (1-inch) balls.

3. Spray large skillet with nonstick cooking spray and heat over medium-high heat. Working in batches, brown meatballs, turning to brown on all sides. Remove to **CROCK-POT**® slow cooker with sauce as batches are done. Cover; cook on HIGH 3 to 4 hours or until meatballs are cooked through.

Chicken Croustade

MAKES 6 TO 8 SERVINGS

2 tablespoons canola oil

1½ pounds boneless, skinless chicken breasts, cut into ¼-inch pieces

Salt and black pepper

1 large portobello mushroom cap

1 shallot, minced

¼ cup dry white wine

1 tablespoon chopped fresh thyme

¼ teaspoon sweet paprika

¼ teaspoon ground cumin

¼ cup chicken broth

1 package (10 ounces) frozen puff pastry shells

1 egg yolk

2 tablespoons whipping cream

3 tablespoons freshly grated Parmesan cheese

Minced fresh chives (optional)

1. Heat oil in large skillet over medium-high heat. Season chicken with salt and pepper; add to skillet. Brown chicken about 4 minutes on each side.

2. Meanwhile, scrape gills from mushroom cap with spoon and discard. Chop mushroom cap into ¼-inch pieces.

3. Remove chicken to **CROCK-POT**® slow cooker. Return skillet to medium-high heat. Add shallot; cook 1 to 2 minutes or until softened. Stir in wine, stirring to scrape up any browned bits from bottom of skillet. Cook until wine is reduced to about 2 tablespoons; pour over chicken. Stir chopped mushroom, thyme, paprika, cumin and broth into **CROCK-POT**® slow cooker. Season with salt and pepper. Cover; cook on LOW 3 hours.

4. Meanwhile, cook puff pastry shells according to package directions. Cool completely.

5. Beat egg yolk and cream in small bowl. Stir 1 tablespoon hot cooking liquid into egg mixture; beat until well combined. Stir egg mixture into remaining cooking liquid. Cook, uncovered, on LOW 20 minutes. Stir in cheese. Divide chicken filling among puff pastry shells. Garnish with chives.

Asian-Spiced Chicken Wings

MAKES 10 TO 16 SERVINGS

3 pounds chicken wings, tips removed

1 cup packed brown sugar

1 cup soy sauce

½ cup ketchup

¼ cup dry sherry

2 teaspoons fresh ginger, minced

2 cloves garlic, minced

½ cup hoisin sauce

1 tablespoon lime juice

3 tablespoons sesame seeds, toasted

¼ cup thinly sliced green onions

1. Preheat broiler. Place wings on broiler pan. Broil wings 4 to 5 inches from heat 10 minutes or until browned. Remove wings to **CROCK-POT**® slow cooker. Stir in brown sugar, soy sauce, ketchup, sherry, ginger and garlic. Cover; cook on LOW 5 to 6 hours or on HIGH 2 to 3 hours, stirring halfway through cooking time.

2. Remove wings with slotted spoon to large serving platter. Remove ¼ cup of cooking liquid; discard remaining liquid. Combine reserved liquid with hoisin sauce and lime juice in medium bowl. Drizzle mixture over wings; sprinkle with sesame seeds and green onions.

NOTE: For 5-, 6- or 7-quart **CROCK-POT**® slow cooker, increase chicken wings to 5 pounds.

Hearty Calico Bean Dip

MAKES 3 CUPS

¾ pound ground beef
1 can (about 15 ounces) baked beans
1 can (about 15 ounces) Great Northern beans, rinsed and drained
1 can (about 15 ounces) kidney beans, rinsed and drained
½ pound bacon, crisp-cooked and crumbled

1 onion, chopped
½ cup packed dark brown sugar
½ cup ketchup
1 tablespoon cider vinegar
1 teaspoon prepared mustard
    Tortilla chips

1. Brown ground beef in large nonstick skillet over medium-high heat 6 to 8 minutes, stirring to break up meat. Drain fat. Remove to **CROCK-POT**® slow cooker.

2. Stir in beans, bacon, onion, brown sugar, ketchup, vinegar and mustard. Cover; cook on LOW 4 hours or on HIGH 2 hours. Serve with tortilla chips.

TIP: For a party, use a small **CROCK-POT**® slow cooker (1 quart or 1½ quarts) on LOW or WARM to keep hot dips warm.

Steamed Pork Buns

MAKES 16 SERVINGS

½ (18-ounce) container refrigerated cooked shredded pork in barbecue sauce*

1 tablespoon Asian garlic chili sauce

1 package (about 16 ounces) refrigerated big biscuit dough (8 biscuits)

Dipping Sauce (recipe follows)

Sliced green onions (optional)

Look for pork in plain, not smoky, barbecue sauce. Substitute chicken in barbecue sauce, if desired.

1. Combine pork and chili sauce in medium bowl. Split biscuits in half. Roll or stretch each biscuit into 4-inch circle. Spoon 1 tablespoon pork onto center of each biscuit. Gather edges around filling and press to seal.

2. Generously butter 2-quart baking dish that fits inside of 5- to 6-quart **CROCK-POT®** slow cooker. Arrange filled biscuits in single layer, overlapping slightly if necessary. Cover dish with buttered foil, butter side down.

3. Place small rack in **CROCK-POT®** slow cooker. Add 1 inch of hot water (water should not touch top of rack). Place baking dish on rack. Cover; cook on HIGH 2 hours.

4. Meanwhile, prepare Dipping Sauce. Garnish pork buns with green onions and serve with Dipping Sauce.

TIP: Straight-sided round casserole or soufflé dishes that fit inside the **CROCK-POT®** stoneware make excellent baking dishes.

DIPPING SAUCE: Stir together 2 tablespoons rice vinegar, 2 tablespoons soy sauce, 4 teaspoons sugar and 1 teaspoon toasted sesame oil in a small bowl until sugar dissolves. Sprinkle with 1 tablespoon minced green onion just before serving.

Angel Wings

MAKES 4 SERVINGS

1 pound chicken wings	¼ cup packed light brown sugar
Salt and black pepper	2½ tablespoons balsamic vinegar
1 can (10¾ ounces) condensed tomato soup, undiluted	2 tablespoons chopped shallots
¾ cup water	

1. Preheat broiler. Place wings on rack in broiler pan; season with salt and pepper. Broil 4 to 5 inches from heat 10 to 12 minutes or until browned, turning once. Remove wings to **CROCK-POT®** slow cooker using slotted spoon.

2. Combine soup, water, brown sugar, vinegar and shallots in small bowl; stir to blend. Pour over wings. Cover; cook on LOW 5 to 6 hours.

> TIP: To reheat leftover foods, don't use the **CROCK-POT®** slow cooker. Remove cooled leftovers to a large resealable food storage bag or storage container with a tight-fitting lid and refrigerate. Use a microwave oven, the stove top or an oven for reheating.

Chunky Veggie Dip

MAKES 3 CUPS

1 red bell pepper, chopped
1 green bell pepper, chopped
½ onion, finely chopped
1 stalk celery, chopped
2 tablespoons water
⅛ teaspoon red pepper flakes
¼ cup milk
¾ teaspoon cornstarch

1 cup (4 ounces) shredded
   sharp Cheddar cheese
2 ounces cream cheese
1 jar (4 ounces) diced
   pimientos
¾ teaspoon salt
   Tortilla chips

1. Coat inside of **CROCK-POT**® slow cooker with nonstick cooking spray. Add bell peppers, onion, celery, water and red pepper flakes. Cover; cook on LOW 3 hours or until celery is tender.

2. Stir milk into cornstarch in small bowl until smooth; add to bell pepper mixture. Add Cheddar cheese and cream cheese, pressing down on cream cheese with rubber spatula until well blended. Stir in pimientos and salt. Cover; cook on LOW 15 minutes or until thickened. Serve with tortilla chips.

VARIATION: Use soft corn tortillas instead of chips. Cut each tortilla into six wedges and bake in a single layer on a baking sheet at 350°F for 10 minutes. Cool completely before serving. Chips will firm as they cool.

Sauced Little Smokies

MAKES 24 SERVINGS

1 bottle (14 ounces) barbecue
   sauce
¾ cup grape jelly
½ cup packed brown sugar
½ cup ketchup

1 tablespoon prepared mustard
1 teaspoon Worcestershire
   sauce
3 packages (14 to 16 ounces
   each) miniature hot dogs

Stir barbecue sauce, jelly, brown sugar, ketchup, mustard and Worcestershire sauce into **CROCK-POT**® slow cooker until combined. Add hot dogs; stir to coat. Cover; cook on LOW 3 to 4 hours or on HIGH 1 to 2 hours.

Beans and Spinach Bruschetta

MAKES 16 SERVINGS

2 cans (about 15 ounces *each*) Great Northern or cannellini beans, rinsed and drained

3 cloves garlic, minced
   Salt and black pepper

6 cups spinach, loosely packed and finely chopped

1 tablespoon red wine vinegar

16 slices whole grain baguette

2 tablespoons extra virgin olive oil

1. Combine beans, garlic, salt and black pepper in **CROCK-POT**® slow cooker; stir to blend. Cover; cook on LOW 3 hours or until beans are tender. Turn off heat. Mash beans with potato masher. Stir in spinach and vinegar.

2. Preheat grill or broiler. Brush baguette slices with oil. Grill 5 to 7 minutes or until bread is golden brown and crisp. Top with bean mixture and spinach.

Cocktail Meatballs

MAKES ABOUT 24 MEATBALLS

1 pound ground beef
1 pound bulk pork or Italian sausage
1 cup cracker crumbs
1 cup finely chopped onion
1 cup finely chopped green bell pepper
½ cup milk
1 egg, beaten
2 teaspoons salt
1 teaspoon Italian seasoning

¼ teaspoon black pepper
1 cup ketchup
¾ cup packed dark brown sugar
½ cup (1 stick) butter or margarine
½ cup cider vinegar
¼ cup lemon juice
¼ cup water
1 teaspoon yellow mustard
¼ teaspoon garlic salt

1. Preheat oven to 350°F. Combine beef, pork, cracker crumbs, onion, bell pepper, milk, egg, salt, Italian seasoning and black pepper in large bowl; mix well. Form into 1-inch meatballs. Place meatballs onto two nonstick baking sheets. Bake 25 minutes or until browned.

2. Meanwhile, place ketchup, brown sugar, butter, vinegar, lemon juice, water, mustard and garlic salt in **CROCK-POT®** slow cooker; mix well. Cover; cook on HIGH 15 to 20 minutes or until heated through.

3. Turn **CROCK-POT®** slow cooker to LOW. Remove meatballs to **CROCK-POT®** slow cooker; carefully stir to coat with sauce. Cover; cook on LOW 2 hours.

Bowls

Southwestern Mac and Cheese

MAKES 6 SERVINGS

1 package (8 ounces)
   uncooked elbow macaroni

1 can (about 14 ounces)
   diced tomatoes with green
   peppers and onions

1 can (10 ounces) diced
   tomatoes with mild green
   chiles

1½ cups salsa

3 cups (12 ounces) shredded
   Mexican cheese blend,
   divided

1. Coat inside of **CROCK-POT**® slow cooker with nonstick cooking spray. Layer macaroni, tomatoes, salsa and 2 cups cheese in **CROCK-POT**® slow cooker. Cover; cook on LOW 3¾ hours.

2. Sprinkle remaining 1 cup cheese over macaroni. Cover; cook on LOW 15 minutes or until cheese is melted.

Corn Chip Chili

MAKES 6 SERVINGS

- 1 tablespoon olive oil
- 1 medium onion, chopped
- 1 medium red bell pepper, chopped
- 1 jalapeño pepper, seeded and finely chopped*
- 4 cloves garlic, minced
- 2 pounds ground beef
- 1 can (4 ounces) diced mild green chiles, drained
- 2 cans (about 14 ounces *each*) fire-roasted diced tomatoes
- 2 tablespoons chili powder
- 1½ teaspoons ground cumin
- 1½ teaspoons dried oregano
- ¾ teaspoon salt
- 3 cups corn chips
- 1 cup (4 ounces) shredded sharp Cheddar cheese
- 6 tablespoons chopped green onions

Jalapeño peppers can sting and irritate the skin, so wear rubber gloves when handling peppers and do not touch your eyes.

1. Coat inside of **CROCK-POT®** slow cooker with nonstick cooking spray.

2. Heat oil in large skillet over medium-high heat. Add onion, bell pepper, jalapeño pepper and garlic; cook and stir 2 minutes or until softened. Add beef; cook and stir 10 to 12 minutes or until beef is no longer pink and liquid has evaporated. Stir in green chiles; cook 1 minute. Remove beef mixture to **CROCK-POT®** slow cooker using slotted spoon. Stir in tomatoes, chili powder, cumin and oregano.

3. Cover; cook on LOW 6 to 7 hours or on HIGH 3½ to 4 hours. Stir in salt. Place corn chips evenly into serving bowls; top with chili. Sprinkle with cheese and green onions.

Leek and Potato Soup

MAKES 4 TO 6 SERVINGS

6 slices bacon, crisp-cooked, chopped and divided

5 cups shredded frozen hash brown potatoes

3 leeks (white and light green parts only), cut into ¾-inch pieces

1 can (about 14 ounces) vegetable broth

1 can (10¾ ounces) condensed cream of potato soup, undiluted

2 stalks celery, sliced

1 can (5 ounces) evaporated milk

½ cup sour cream

Set aside 2 tablespoons bacon. Combine remaining bacon, potatoes, leeks, broth, soup, celery and evaporated milk in **CROCK-POT**® slow cooker. Cover; cook on LOW 6 to 7 hours. Stir in sour cream. Sprinkle each serving with reserved bacon.

Ghormeh Sabzi (Persian Green Stew)

MAKES 6 SERVINGS

1½ pounds boneless leg of lamb, cut into 1-inch cubes
1 teaspoon ground turmeric
½ teaspoon salt
½ teaspoon curry powder
¼ teaspoon black pepper
2 tablespoons olive oil, divided
2 medium onions, chopped
1 package (5 ounces) baby spinach, chopped
2 cups chopped fresh Italian parsley

1 cup chopped fresh cilantro
6 green onions, (green part only), chopped
1½ cups beef broth
1 can (about 15 ounces) cannellini beans, rinsed and drained
2 tablespoons lime juice
3 cups hot cooked basmati rice
Naan bread (optional)

1. Coat inside of **CROCK-POT®** slow cooker with nonstick cooking spray.

2. Combine lamb, turmeric, salt, curry powder and pepper in large bowl. Heat 1 tablespoon oil in large skillet over medium-high heat. Add half of lamb; cook and stir 4 minutes or until browned. Remove to **CROCK-POT®** slow cooker. Repeat with remaining lamb. Add onions and remaining 1 tablespoon oil to skillet; cook 6 to 7 minutes or until onions are starting to brown. Stir in spinach, parsley, cilantro and green onions; cook and stir 2 minutes or until spinach is wilted. Add to lamb in **CROCK-POT®** slow cooker; pour broth over all.

3. Cover; cook on LOW 8 hours or on HIGH 4 hours. Add beans. Cover; cook on HIGH 30 minutes. Turn off heat. Stir in lime juice. Serve with rice and naan, if desired.

Shrimp and Okra Gumbo

MAKES 6 SERVINGS

1 tablespoon olive oil

8 ounces kielbasa, halved lengthwise and cut into ¼-inch-thick half slices

1 green bell pepper, chopped

1 medium onion, chopped

3 stalks celery, cut into ¼-inch slices

6 green onions, chopped

4 cloves garlic, minced

1 cup chicken broth

1 can (about 14 ounces) diced tomatoes

1 teaspoon Cajun seasoning

½ teaspoon dried thyme

1 pound large raw shrimp, peeled and deveined (with tails on)

2 cups frozen cut okra, thawed

1. Coat inside of **CROCK-POT**® slow cooker with nonstick cooking spray. Heat oil in large skillet over medium-high heat. Add kielbasa; cook and stir 4 minutes or until browned. Remove to **CROCK-POT**® slow cooker using slotted spoon.

2. Return skillet to medium-high heat. Add bell pepper, chopped onion, celery, green onions and garlic; cook and stir 5 to 6 minutes or until vegetables are crisp-tender. Remove to **CROCK-POT**® slow cooker. Stir in broth, tomatoes, Cajun seasoning and thyme.

3. Cover; cook on LOW 4 hours. Stir in shrimp and okra. Cover; cook on LOW 30 to 35 minutes.

Sweet Potato and Black Bean Chipotle Chili

MAKES 8 TO 10 SERVINGS

1 tablespoon vegetable oil

2 large onions, diced

1 tablespoon minced garlic

2 tablespoons tomato paste

3 tablespoons chili powder

1 tablespoon chipotle chili powder

1 teaspoon ground cumin

2 teaspoons salt

1 cup water

2 large sweet potatoes, peeled and cut into ½-inch pieces (about 2 pounds)

2 cans (15 ounces *each*) black beans, rinsed and drained

2 cans (28 ounces *each*) crushed tomatoes

Optional toppings: sliced green onions, shredded Cheddar cheese and/or tortilla chips

1. Heat oil in large skillet over medium-high heat. Add onions; cook 8 minutes or until lightly browned and softened. Add garlic, tomato paste, chili powder, chipotle chili powder, cumin and salt; cook and stir 1 minute. Add water, stirring to scrape up any brown bits from bottom of skillet. Remove to **CROCK-POT**® slow cooker. Add sweet potatoes, beans and tomatoes.

2. Cover; cook on LOW 8 hours or on HIGH 4 hours. Ladle into individual bowls. Top with desired toppings.

Cheesy Tavern Soup

MAKES 8 SERVINGS

2 tablespoons olive oil
½ cup chopped celery
½ cup chopped carrot
½ cup chopped onion
½ cup chopped green bell
  pepper
8 cups chicken broth
2 cans (12 ounces *each*) beer, at
  room temperature

¼ cup (½ stick) butter
2 teaspoons salt
2 teaspoons black pepper
½ cup all-purpose flour
4 cups (16 ounces) shredded
  Cheddar cheese
Sliced green onions
  (optional)

1. Heat oil in medium skillet over medium heat. Add celery, carrot, chopped onion and bell pepper; cook and stir 3 to 5 minutes or until tender. Remove to **CROCK-POT®** slow cooker.

2. Add broth, beer, butter, salt and black pepper to **CROCK-POT®** slow cooker. Cover; cook on LOW 6 hours or on HIGH 2 to 4 hours.

3. Stir small amount of water into flour in small bowl until smooth. Whisk into **CROCK-POT®** slow cooker. Cover; cook on HIGH 10 to 15 minutes or until thickened.

4. Preheat broiler. Ladle soup into individual broiler-safe bowls. Top each with ½ cup cheese. Broil 10 to 15 minutes or until cheese is melted. Garnish with green onions.

Chicken Congee

MAKES 6 SERVINGS

6 cups water
4 cups chicken broth
4 chicken drumsticks
1 cup uncooked white jasmine rice, rinsed and drained
1 (1-inch) piece fresh ginger, sliced into 4 pieces
2 teaspoons salt

¼ teaspoon ground white pepper
Optional toppings: soy sauce, sesame oil, thinly sliced green onions, fried shallots, fried garlic slices, salted roasted peanuts and/or pickled vegetables

1. Add water, broth, chicken, rice, ginger, salt and pepper to **CROCK-POT**® slow cooker. Cover; cook on LOW 8 hours or on HIGH 4 hours or until rice has completely broken down and mixture is thickened.

2. Remove and discard ginger. Remove chicken to large cutting board. Discard skin and bones. Shred chicken using two forks. Stir chicken back into **CROCK-POT**® slow cooker. Ladle congee into serving bowls; top with desired toppings.

Traditional Cassoulet

MAKES 4 SERVINGS

1 can (about 15 ounces) cannellini beans, rinsed and drained

½ cup finely chopped carrots

½ cup roughly chopped seeded tomatoes

1 small onion, finely chopped

¼ cup plain dry bread crumbs

2 cloves garlic, finely chopped

2 tablespoons finely chopped fresh marjoram

2 tablespoons finely chopped fresh Italian parsley

2 tablespoons olive oil

1½ pounds chicken thighs

½ pound bulk pork sausage

½ cup dry white wine

½ cup chicken broth

1. Combine beans, carrots, tomatoes, onion, bread crumbs, garlic, marjoram and parsley in **CROCK-POT**® slow cooker.

2. Heat oil in large skillet over medium-high heat. Add chicken, working in batches, if necessary; cook 3 to 4 minutes per side or until brown. Place chicken on top of onion mixture in **CROCK-POT**® slow cooker. Add sausage to skillet. Brown 6 to 8 minutes, stirring to break up meat. Drain fat. Remove sausage to **CROCK-POT**® slow cooker.

3. Return skillet to medium-high heat. Add wine and broth, stirring to scrape up any browned bits from bottom of skillet. Bring to a boil; cook until liquid is reduced to about one third. Remove from heat.

4. Pour reduced liquid over contents of **CROCK-POT**® slow cooker. Cover; cook on LOW 6 to 7 hours or on HIGH 3 to 4 hours.

Slow-Cooked Shakshuka

MAKES 6 SERVINGS

¼ cup extra virgin olive oil

1 medium onion, chopped

1 large red bell pepper, chopped

3 cloves garlic, sliced

1 can (28 ounces) crushed tomatoes with basil, garlic and oregano

2 teaspoons paprika

2 teaspoons ground cumin

2 teaspoons sugar

½ teaspoon salt

¼ teaspoon red pepper flakes

¾ cup crumbled feta cheese

6 eggs

Chopped fresh cilantro (optional)

Black pepper (optional)

Toasted baguette slices (optional)

1. Spray inside of **CROCK-POT**® slow cooker with nonstick cooking spray. Combine oil, onion, bell pepper, garlic, tomatoes, paprika, cumin, sugar, salt and red pepper flakes in **CROCK-POT**® slow cooker; stir to blend. Cover; cook on HIGH 3 hours. Stir in feta cheese; break eggs, one at a time, onto top of tomato mixture, leaving a little space between each.

2. Cover; cook on HIGH 15 to 18 minutes or until the egg whites are set but yolks are still creamy. Scoop eggs and sauce evenly into each serving bowl. Garnish with cilantro and black pepper. Serve with baguette slices, if desired.

Pesto, White Bean and Pasta Stew

MAKES 6 SERVINGS

1 can (28 ounces) Italian seasoned diced tomatoes

2 cups vegetable broth

1 green bell pepper, cut into pieces

1 cup uncooked elbow macaroni or ditalini pasta

1 can (about 15 ounces) cannellini or Great Northern beans, rinsed and drained

¼ cup prepared basil pesto

⅓ cup grated Parmesan or Romano cheese

1. Coat inside of **CROCK-POT®** slow cooker with nonstick cooking spray. Combine tomatoes, broth, bell pepper and pasta in **CROCK-POT®** slow cooker. Cover; cook on LOW 4 to 5 hours or on HIGH 2 to 3 hours.

2. Stir in beans and pesto. Cover; cook on HIGH 10 to 15 minutes or until heated through. Ladle into shallow bowls; top with cheese.

Hearty Sausage and Tortellini Soup

MAKES 6 TO 8 SERVINGS

3 hot Italian sausages, casings removed

3 sweet Italian sausages, casings removed

5 cups chicken broth

1 can (about 14 ounces) diced tomatoes with garlic and oregano

1 can (about 8 ounces) tomato sauce

1 large onion, chopped

2 medium carrots, chopped

1 teaspoon seasoned salt

½ teaspoon Italian seasoning

¼ teaspoon black pepper

1 package (9 ounces) refrigerated cheese tortellini

1 medium zucchini, chopped

2 cups broccoli, chopped

1. Cook sausages in large skillet over medium-high heat 8 to 10 minutes, stirring to break up meat. Drain fat. Add sausages, broth, diced tomatoes, tomato sauce, onion, carrots, seasoned salt, Italian seasoning and pepper to **CROCK-POT**® slow cooker. Cover; cook on LOW 6 to 8 hours or on HIGH 3 to 4 hours.

2. Meanwhile, cook tortellini according to package directions. Add tortellini, zucchini and broccoli to **CROCK-POT**® slow cooker during last 15 to 20 minutes of cooking.

Mole Chili

MAKES 4 TO 6 SERVINGS

2 corn tortillas, each cut into 4 wedges

1½ pounds beef chuck roast, cut into 1-inch pieces

¾ teaspoon salt, divided

½ teaspoon black pepper, divided

3 tablespoons olive oil, divided

2 medium onions, chopped

5 cloves garlic, minced

1 cup beef broth

1 can (about 14 ounces) fire-roasted diced tomatoes

2 tablespoons chili powder

1 tablespoon ground ancho chile

1 teaspoon ground cumin

1 teaspoon dried oregano

¾ teaspoon ground cinnamon

1 can (about 15 ounces) red kidney beans, rinsed and drained

2 ounces semisweet chocolate, chopped

Queso fresco (optional)

Chopped fresh cilantro (optional)

1. Coat inside of **CROCK-POT®** slow cooker with nonstick cooking spray. Place tortillas in food processor or blender; process to fine crumbs. Set aside.

2. Season beef with salt and pepper. Heat 1 tablespoon oil in large skillet over medium-high heat. Add half of beef to skillet; cook 4 minutes or until browned. Remove to **CROCK-POT®** slow cooker. Add 1 tablespoon oil to skillet; repeat with remaining beef. Heat remaining 1 tablespoon oil in skillet. Add onions and garlic; cook 2 minutes or until onions begin to soften. Pour broth into skillet, scraping up any browned bits from bottom of skillet. Remove to **CROCK-POT®** slow cooker. Stir in reserved tortilla crumbs, tomatoes, chili powder, ancho chile, cumin, oregano and cinnamon.

3. Cover; cook on LOW 8 to 8½ hours or on HIGH 4 to 4½ hours. Stir in beans. Cover; cook on LOW 30 minutes. Turn off heat. Add chocolate, remaining ¼ teaspoon salt and ¼ teaspoon pepper; stir until chocolate is melted. Top with queso fresco and cilantro, if desired.

Fall Harvest Stew

MAKES 8 SERVINGS

2½ pounds cubed beef stew meat

¼ cup all-purpose flour

2 tablespoons olive oil

1 tablespoon butter

1 medium onion, chopped

1 head garlic, minced

2 whole bay leaves

1 tablespoon fresh rosemary, chopped

1½ teaspoons fresh thyme, chopped

½ cup beef broth, divided

1 pound carrots, cut into 2-inch pieces

4 turnips, cut into 1-inch pieces

1 butternut squash, cut into 2-inch pieces

1 can (12 ounces) stout, divided

⅛ teaspoon white pepper

Dash apple pie spice

Salt and black pepper

1. Place beef and flour in large bowl; toss to coat beef. Heat oil and butter in large skillet over medium-high heat. Add beef; brown on all sides. Remove to **CROCK-POT**® slow cooker.

2. Return skillet to heat. Add onion, garlic, bay leaves, rosemary and thyme; cook until onion begins to soften. Add mixture to **CROCK-POT**® slow cooker.

3. Return skillet to heat. Add ¼ cup broth; deglaze pan. Add broth mixture, carrots, turnips, squash, stout, white pepper and apple pie spice to **CROCK-POT**® slow cooker. Season with salt and black pepper. Add remaining ¼ cup broth. Cover; cook on LOW 8 hours. Remove and discard bay leaves before serving.

Koshari

MAKES 6 TO 8 SERVINGS

6 cups water

1 cup uncooked white basmati rice, rinsed and drained

1 cup brown lentils, rinsed and sorted

3 teaspoons salt, divided

1 teaspoon ground cinnamon, divided

½ teaspoon ground nutmeg, divided

1 cup uncooked elbow macaroni

¼ cup olive oil

1 large onion, thinly sliced

1 large onion, diced

1 tablespoon minced garlic

1 teaspoon ground cumin

½ teaspoon ground coriander

¼ teaspoon red pepper flakes

¼ teaspoon black pepper

1 can (28 ounces) crushed tomatoes

2 teaspoons red wine vinegar

1. Place water, rice, lentils, 2 teaspoons salt, ½ teaspoon cinnamon and ¼ teaspoon nutmeg in **CROCK-POT**® slow cooker. Cover; cook on HIGH 2 to 3 hours. Stir in macaroni. Cover; cook on HIGH 30 minutes, stirring halfway through cooking time.

2. Meanwhile, heat oil in large skillet over medium-high heat. Add sliced onion; cook 12 minutes or until edges are dark brown and onion is softened. Remove onion to medium bowl using slotted spoon. Season with ¼ teaspoon salt. Set aside.

3. Heat same skillet with oil over medium heat. Add diced onion; cook 8 minutes or until softened. Add garlic, cumin, coriander, remaining ½ teaspoon cinnamon, red pepper flakes, black pepper and remaining ¼ teaspoon nutmeg; cook 30 seconds or until fragrant. Stir in tomatoes and remaining ¾ teaspoon salt; cook 8 to 10 minutes or until thickened, stirring occasionally. Stir in vinegar.

4. Fluff rice mixture lightly before scooping into individual bowls. Top each serving evenly with tomato sauce and reserved onions.

Sweet and Sour Shrimp with Pineapple

MAKES 4 SERVINGS

3 cans (8 ounces *each*) pineapple chunks

2 packages (6 ounces *each*) frozen snow peas

⅓ cup plus 2 teaspoons sugar

¼ cup cornstarch

2 cubes chicken bouillon

2 cups boiling water

4 teaspoons soy sauce

1 teaspoon ground ginger

1 pound medium raw shrimp, peeled and deveined (with tails on)*

¼ cup cider vinegar

Hot cooked rice

Or 1 pound frozen medium raw shrimp, peeled, deveined and unthawed.

1. Drain pineapple chunks, reserving 1 cup juice. Place pineapple and snow peas in **CROCK-POT**® slow cooker.

2. Combine sugar and cornstarch in medium saucepan. Dissolve bouillon cubes in boiling water in small bowl; add to saucepan. Mix in reserved pineapple juice, soy sauce and ginger; bring to a boil and cook 1 minute. Pour mixture into **CROCK-POT**® slow cooker. Cover; cook on LOW 4½ to 5½ hours.

3. Add shrimp and vinegar. Cover; cook on LOW 30 minutes or until shrimp are cooked through. Serve over rice.

Paella

MAKES 8 SERVINGS

4 cups boneless, skinless chicken breasts, cut into 1-inch cubes

1 cup chopped onion

1 cup chopped tomatoes

4 teaspoons chopped pimientos

1 teaspoon salt

1 teaspoon black pepper

½ teaspoon dried oregano

¼ teaspoon saffron threads

4 cups cooked rice

4 cups shucked whole clams or canned clams

1 pound large raw shrimp, peeled and deveined (with tails on)

1 cup or 2 cans (8 ounces *each*) lobster meat

8 ounces scallops

1. Place chicken, onion, tomatoes, pimientos, salt, pepper, oregano and saffron in **CROCK-POT**® slow cooker. Cover; cook on LOW 6 hours or on HIGH 2 to 4 hours.

2. Add rice, clams, shrimp, lobster and scallops. Cover; cook on HIGH 15 minutes or until shrimp and scallops are pink and opague.

Thai Red Curry with Tofu

MAKES 4 SERVINGS

1 medium sweet potato, peeled and cut into 1-inch pieces

1 small eggplant, halved lengthwise and cut crosswise into ½-inch-wide halves

8 ounces extra firm tofu, cut into 1-inch pieces

½ cup green beans, cut into 1-inch pieces

½ red bell pepper, cut into ¼-inch-wide strips

2 tablespoons vegetable oil

5 medium shallots (about 1½ cups), thinly sliced

3 tablespoons Thai red curry paste

1 teaspoon minced garlic

1 teaspoon grated ginger

1 can (about 13 ounces) unsweetened coconut milk

1½ tablespoons soy sauce

1 tablespoon packed light brown sugar

¼ cup chopped fresh basil

2 tablespoons lime juice

Hot cooked rice (optional)

1. Coat inside of **CROCK-POT**® slow cooker with nonstick cooking spray. Add potato, eggplant, tofu, beans and bell pepper.

2. Heat oil in large skillet over medium heat. Add shallots; cook 5 minutes or until browned and tender. Add curry paste, garlic and ginger; cook and stir 1 minute. Add coconut milk, soy sauce and brown sugar; bring to a simmer. Pour mixture over vegetables in **CROCK-POT**® slow cooker.

3. Cover; cook on LOW 2 to 3 hours. Stir in basil and lime juice. Serve over rice, if desired.

Turkey Italian Sausage with White Beans

MAKES 4 SERVINGS

1 pound turkey or pork Italian sausage, casings removed

½ cup minced onion

2 cans (about 15 ounces *each*) cannellini or Great Northern beans, rinsed and drained

1 can (about 14 ounces) Italian seasoned diced tomatoes

1 teaspoon dried rosemary

½ cup grated Parmesan or Romano cheese

1. Heat large skillet over medium-high heat. Brown sausage and onion 6 to 8 minutes, stirring to break up meat. Drain fat.

2. Coat inside of **CROCK-POT®** slow cooker with nonstick cooking spray. Combine beans, tomatoes and rosemary in **CROCK-POT®** slow cooker. Stir in sausage mixture. Cover; cook on LOW 3 to 4 hours or on HIGH 1½ to 2 hours. Ladle into bowls; top with cheese.

Country Chicken and Vegetables with Creamy Herb Sauce

MAKES 4 SERVINGS

1 pound new potatoes, cut into ½-inch wedges

1 medium onion, cut into 8 wedges

½ cup coarsely chopped celery

4 bone-in chicken drumsticks, skinned

4 bone-in chicken thighs, skinned

1 can (10¾ ounces) cream of chicken soup

1 packet (1 ounce) ranch-style dressing mix

½ teaspoon dried thyme

¼ teaspoon black pepper

½ cup whipping cream

Salt

¼ cup finely chopped green onions (green and white parts)

1. Coat inside of **CROCK-POT**® slow cooker with nonstick cooking spray. Arrange potatoes, onion and celery in bottom. Add chicken. Combine soup, dressing mix, thyme and pepper in small bowl. Spoon mixture evenly over chicken and vegetables. Cover; cook on HIGH 3½ hours.

2. Remove chicken to shallow serving bowl with slotted spoon. Add cream and salt, if desired, to cooking liquid. Stir well to blend. Pour sauce over chicken. Garnish with green onions.

NOTE: To skin chicken easily, grasp skin with paper towel and pull away. Repeat with fresh paper towel for each piece of chicken, discarding skins and towels.

Scallops in Fresh Tomato and Herb Sauce

MAKES 4 SERVINGS

- 2 tablespoons vegetable oil
- 1 medium red onion, peeled and diced
- 1 clove garlic, minced
- 3½ cups fresh tomatoes, peeled*
- 1 can (12 ounces) tomato pureé
- 1 can (6 ounces) tomato paste
- ¼ cup dry red wine
- 2 tablespoons chopped fresh Italian parsley
- 1 tablespoon chopped fresh oregano
- ¼ teaspoon black pepper
- 1½ pounds fresh scallops, cleaned and drained

Hot cooked pasta or rice

*To peel tomatoes, place one at a time in simmering water about 10 seconds. (Add 30 seconds if tomatoes are not fully ripened.) Immediately plunge into a bowl of cold water for another 10 seconds. Peel skin with a knife.

1. Heat oil in medium skillet over medium heat. Add onion and garlic; cook and stir 7 to 8 minutes or until onion is soft and translucent. Remove to **CROCK-POT**® slow cooker.

2. Add tomatoes, tomato purée, tomato paste, wine, parsley, oregano and pepper. Cover; cook on LOW 6 to 8 hours.

3. Turn **CROCK-POT**® slow cooker to HIGH. Add scallops. Cook on HIGH 15 minutes or until scallops are opaque. Serve over pasta.

Salmon Chowder

MAKES 6 SERVINGS

1 can (about 15 ounces) cream-style corn

1 can (about 14 ounces) chicken broth

8 ounces small red potatoes, chopped

1 red onion, finely chopped

¼ teaspoon salt

½ teaspoon black pepper

1 package (8 ounces) cream cheese

½ teaspoon grated lemon peel

1 salmon fillet (about 1½ pounds), skinned and cut into 6 pieces

⅓ cup chopped fresh dill (optional)

Lemon wedges (optional)

1. Combine corn, broth, potatoes, onion, salt and pepper in **CROCK-POT®** slow cooker; stir to blend. Cover; cook on LOW 4 hours or on HIGH 2 hours.

2. Whisk cream cheese and lemon peel into **CROCK-POT®** slow cooker until smooth. Top with salmon. Cover; cook on LOW 45 minutes to 1 hour or until fillets begin to flake when tested with fork. Remove fillets from **CROCK-POT®** slow cooker. Ladle soup into bowls; top each with salmon fillet. Garnish with dill and lemon wedge.

Mexican Hot Pot

MAKES 6 SERVINGS

1 tablespoon canola oil
1 medium onion, chopped
3 cloves garlic, minced
2 teaspoons red pepper flakes
2 teaspoons dried oregano
1 teaspoon ground cumin
1 can (28 ounces) whole tomatoes, drained and chopped

2 cups corn
1 can (about 15 ounces) chickpeas, rinsed and drained
1 can (about 15 ounces) pinto beans, rinsed and drained
1 cup water
1½ cups shredded iceberg lettuce

1. Heat oil in large skillet over medium-high heat. Add onion and garlic; cook and stir 5 minutes. Add red pepper flakes, oregano and cumin; mix well. Remove onion and garlic mixture to **CROCK-POT®** slow cooker.

2. Stir in tomatoes, corn, chickpeas, beans and water. Cover; cook on LOW 7 to 8 hours or on HIGH 3 to 4 hours. Top each serving with ¼ cup shredded lettuce.

Mediterranean Meatball Ratatouille

MAKES 6 SERVINGS

1 pound bulk mild Italian sausage

1 package (8 ounces) sliced mushrooms

1 small eggplant, diced

1 zucchini, diced

½ cup chopped yellow onion

1 clove garlic, minced

1 teaspoon dried oregano

1 teaspoon salt

½ teaspoon black pepper

2 tomatoes, diced

1 tablespoon tomato paste

2 tablespoons chopped fresh basil

1 teaspoon fresh lemon juice

1. Shape sausage into 1-inch meatballs. Brown meatballs in large skillet over medium heat. Place half of the meatballs in **CROCK-POT**® slow cooker. Add half *each* of mushrooms, eggplant and zucchini. Top with onion, garlic, ½ teaspoon oregano, ½ teaspoon salt and ¼ teaspoon pepper.

2. Add remaining meatballs, mushrooms, eggplant, zucchini, ½ teaspoon oregano, ½ teaspoon salt and ¼ teaspoon pepper. Cover; cook on LOW 6 to 7 hours.

3. Stir diced tomatoes and tomato paste into **CROCK-POT**® slow cooker. Cover; cook on LOW 15 minutes. Stir in basil and lemon juice just before serving.

Entrées

Miso-Poached Salmon

MAKES 6 SERVINGS

1½ cups water
2 green onions, cut into 2-inch long pieces, plus additional for garnish
¼ cup yellow miso paste
¼ cup soy sauce
2 tablespoons sake

2 tablespoons mirin
1½ teaspoons grated fresh ginger
1 teaspoon minced garlic
6 salmon fillets (4 ounces *each*)
Hot cooked rice (optional)

1. Combine water, 2 green onions, miso paste, soy sauce, sake, mirin, ginger and garlic in **CROCK-POT**® slow cooker; stir to blend. Cover; cook on HIGH 30 minutes.

2. Turn **CROCK-POT**® slow cooker to LOW. Add salmon, skin side down. Cover; cook on LOW 30 minutes to 1 hour or until salmon begins to flake easily when tested with fork. Serve over rice with cooking liquid as desired. Garnish with additional green onions.

Turkey Meat Loaf

MAKES 6 TO 8 SERVINGS

1 pound ground white meat turkey

1 pound ground dark meat turkey

1 can (about 14 ounces) diced tomatoes, drained

1 medium onion, chopped

1 medium green bell pepper, chopped

1 cup seasoned dry bread crumbs

¼ cup ketchup, plus additional for topping

2 tablespoons yellow mustard

2 eggs

2 teaspoons garlic powder

2 teaspoons dried oregano

2 teaspoons dried basil

2 teaspoons Worcestershire sauce

1 teaspoon salt

½ teaspoon black pepper

2 tablespoons packed brown sugar (optional)

1. Coat inside of **CROCK-POT®** slow cooker with nonstick cooking spray. Prepare foil handles by tearing off four 18×2-inch strips heavy foil (or use regular foil folded to double thickness). Crisscross foil strips in spoke design; place in round **CROCK-POT®** slow cooker. Spray foil handles with nonstick cooking spray.

2. Combine turkey meat, tomatoes, onion, bell pepper, bread crumbs, ¼ cup ketchup, mustard, eggs, garlic powder, oregano, basil, Worcestershire sauce, salt and black pepper in large bowl; mix well. Form mixture into loaf. Place loaf on top of foil in **CROCK-POT®** slow cooker. Spread top of meat loaf with additional ketchup and brown sugar, if desired. Cover; cook on LOW 7 to 8 hours or on HIGH 3 to 4 hours. Remove meat loaf from **CROCK-POT®** slow cooker using foil handles to large cutting board. Let stand 10 minutes before slicing.

Sweet Jalapeño Mustard Turkey Thighs

MAKES 6 SERVINGS

6 turkey thighs, skin removed
¾ cup honey mustard
½ cup orange juice
1 to 2 fresh jalapeño peppers, seeded and finely chopped*
1 tablespoon cider vinegar
1 teaspoon Worcestershire sauce

1 clove garlic, minced
½ teaspoon grated orange peel

Jalapeño peppers can sting and irritate the skin, so wear rubber gloves when handling peppers and do not touch your eyes.

Combine turkey, mustard, orange juice, jalapeño peppers, vinegar, Worcestershire sauce, garlic and orange peel in **CROCK-POT®** slow cooker. Cover; cook on LOW 5 to 6 hours.

Creamy Mushroom Stroganoff

MAKES 4 SERVINGS

3 tablespoons unsalted butter

2 medium onions, sliced

2½ pounds white button mushrooms, thickly sliced

1 teaspoon dried thyme

¾ teaspoon salt, divided

½ teaspoon black pepper, divided

6 cloves garlic, minced

⅓ cup dry white wine

1 cup vegetable broth

2 teaspoons Worcestershire sauce

2 teaspoons Dijon mustard

⅔ cup sour cream

2 tablespoons chopped fresh Italian parsley

8 ounces extra wide egg noodles, cooked and drained

1. Coat inside of **CROCK-POT®** slow cooker with nonstick cooking spray. Melt butter in large skillet over medium-high heat. Add onions, half of mushrooms, thyme, ½ teaspoon salt and ¼ teaspoon pepper; cook and stir 3 minutes or until mushrooms have cooked down slightly. Add remaining mushrooms. Cook 15 minutes or until mushrooms are tender and liquid has almost completely evaporated. Add garlic; cook 2 minutes. Pour in wine; cook and stir 1 minute. Remove to **CROCK-POT®** slow cooker. Stir in broth, Worcestershire sauce and mustard.

2. Cover; cook on LOW 4 to 4½ hours or on HIGH 2 to 2½ hours. Turn off heat. Let cool 10 minutes. Stir in sour cream, parsley and remaining ¼ teaspoon salt and ¼ teaspoon pepper. Divide noodles evenly among four plates; top with stroganoff to serve.

Spanish Paella with Chicken and Sausage

MAKES 4 SERVINGS

1 tablespoon olive oil

4 chicken thighs (about 2 pounds *total*)

1 medium onion, chopped

4 cups chicken broth

1 pound hot smoked sausage, sliced into rounds

1 can (about 14 ounces) stewed tomatoes, undrained

1 cup uncooked Arborio rice

1 clove garlic, minced

1 pinch saffron threads (optional)

½ cup frozen peas, thawed

1. Heat oil in large skillet over medium-high heat. Add chicken in batches; cook 6 to 8 minutes until browned well on all sides. Remove chicken to **CROCK-POT**® slow cooker as it browns.

2. Add onion to same skillet; cook until translucent. Stir broth, sausage, tomatoes, rice and garlic into skillet. Stir in saffron, if desired. Pour over chicken in **CROCK-POT**® slow cooker. Cover; cook on LOW 6 to 8 hours or on HIGH 3 to 4 hours or until chicken is fully cooked and rice is tender.

3. Remove chicken pieces to large plate; fluff rice with fork. Stir peas into rice. Spoon rice into bowls; top with chicken.

Tuscan-Style Lamb Shanks

MAKES 4 SERVINGS

4 lamb shanks (12 to 14 ounces *each*), trimmed
  Salt and black pepper
1 tablespoon extra virgin olive oil
1 medium onion, chopped (about 1 cup)
2 stalks celery, chopped
2 carrots, chopped

4 cloves garlic, minced
2 teaspoons dried sage
1 teaspoon dried rosemary
1 can (28 ounces) crushed tomatoes with basil
3 tablespoons tomato paste
  Hot cooked fettuccine

1. Coat inside of **CROCK-POT**® slow cooker with nonstick cooking spray. Season lamb with salt and pepper. Heat oil in large skillet over medium-high heat. Add lamb in batches; cook 8 to 10 minutes or until well browned, turning occasionally. Remove lamb to **CROCK-POT**® slow cooker.

2. Return skillet to heat. Add onion, celery, carrots, garlic, sage and rosemary; cook and stir 2 to 3 minutes or until vegetables are just starting to soften. Stir in tomatoes, tomato paste, salt and pepper; cook 1 minute. Pour tomato mixture over lamb shanks in **CROCK-POT**® slow cooker.

3. Cover; cook on LOW 7 to 8 hours or on HIGH 3 to 4 hours. Serve lamb over fettuccine with sauce.

Three Onion Chicken

MAKES 6 SERVINGS

3 tablespoons butter

3 onions, chopped

3 leeks (white and light green parts only), sliced

2 cloves garlic, chopped

½ cup dry white wine

2 tablespoons lemon juice

½ cup chicken broth

6 boneless, skinless chicken breasts (6 ounces *each*)

1 teaspoon salt

¼ teaspoon black pepper

½ teaspoon dried thyme

2 green onions, sliced

1. Melt butter in large skillet over medium-high heat. Add onions; cook and stir 3 to 5 minutes or until translucent. Add leeks; cook and stir 5 minutes or until onions are golden brown and leeks are tender. Add garlic; cook and stir 30 seconds. Add wine and lemon juice; cook and stir until most liquid is evaporated. Remove to **CROCK-POT**® slow cooker. Pour in broth.

2. Sprinkle chicken with salt and pepper. Add chicken to **CROCK-POT**® slow cooker. Sprinkle with thyme. Cover; cook on HIGH 1½ hours or until chicken is cooked through. Sprinkle with green onions before serving.

Zesty Chicken and Rice Supper

MAKES 3 TO 4 SERVINGS

2 boneless, skinless chicken breasts, cut into 1-inch pieces

2 large green bell peppers, coarsely chopped

1 small onion, chopped

1 can (about 28 ounces) diced tomatoes

1 cup uncooked converted long grain white rice

1 cup water

1 package (about 1 ounce) taco seasoning mix

1 teaspoon salt

1 teaspoon black pepper

1 teaspoon ground red pepper

Shredded Cheddar cheese (optional)

Combine chicken, bell peppers, onion, tomatoes, rice, water, taco seasoning mix, salt, black pepper and ground red pepper in **CROCK-POT®** slow cooker; stir to blend. Cover; cook on LOW 6 to 8 hours or on HIGH 3 to 4 hours. Garnish with cheese.

Thai-Style Chicken Thighs

MAKES 6 SERVINGS

1 teaspoon ground ginger

½ teaspoon salt

¼ teaspoon ground red pepper

6 bone-in chicken thighs
(about 2¼ pounds *total*),
skin removed

1 onion, chopped

3 cloves garlic, minced

⅓ cup canned unsweetened
coconut milk

¼ cup peanut butter

2 tablespoons soy sauce

2 tablespoons water

1 tablespoon cornstarch

3 cups hot cooked couscous or
yellow rice

¼ cup chopped fresh cilantro

Lime wedges (optional)

1. Combine ginger, salt and ground red pepper in small bowl; sprinkle over chicken. Place onion and garlic in **CROCK-POT**® slow cooker; top with chicken. Stir coconut milk, peanut butter and soy sauce in small bowl; pour over chicken. Cover; cook on LOW 6 to 7 hours or on HIGH 3 to 4 hours. Remove chicken to serving bowl. Cover loosely with foil.

2. Stir water into cornstarch in small bowl until smooth; whisk into **CROCK-POT**® slow cooker. Cover; cook on HIGH 15 minutes or until sauce is slightly thickened. Spoon sauce over chicken. Serve chicken over couscous; top with cilantro. Garnish with lime wedges.

Simple Slow Cooker Pork Roast

MAKES 6 SERVINGS

4 to 5 red potatoes, halved

4 carrots, sliced into 1-inch pieces

1 marinated pork loin roast (3 to 4 pounds)*

½ cup water

1 package (10 ounces) frozen baby peas

Salt and black pepper

Sprigs fresh rosemary and sage (optional)

If marinated roast is unavailable, combine ¼ cup olive oil, 1 tablespoon minced garlic and 1½ tablespoons Italian seasoning in large resealable food storage bag. Add pork; turn to coat. Marinate in refrigerator at least 2 hours or overnight.

1. Layer potatoes, carrots and pork roast in **CROCK-POT**® slow cooker. (If necessary, cut roast in half to fit.) Add water. Cover; cook on LOW 6 to 8 hours.

2. Add peas during last hour of cooking. Remove pork to large serving platter. Season with salt and pepper. Garnish with rosemary and sage. Slice and serve with vegetables.

Tuna Casserole

MAKES 6 SERVINGS

2 cans (10¾ ounces *each*) cream of celery soup

2 cans (5 ounces *each*) tuna in water, drained and flaked

1 cup water

2 carrots, chopped

1 small red onion, chopped

¼ teaspoon black pepper

1 raw egg, uncracked

8 ounces hot cooked egg noodles

Plain dry bread crumbs

2 tablespoons chopped fresh Italian parsley

1. Stir soup, tuna, water, carrots, onion and pepper into **CROCK-POT®** slow cooker. Place whole unpeeled egg on top. Cover; cook on LOW 4 to 5 hours or on HIGH 2 to 3 hours.

2. Remove egg; stir in pasta. Cover; cook on HIGH 30 to 60 minutes or until onion is tender. Meanwhile, mash egg in small bowl; mix in bread crumbs and parsley. Top casserole with bread crumb mixture.

NOTE: This casserole calls for a raw egg. The egg will hard-cook in its shell in the **CROCK-POT®** slow cooker.

Easy Salisbury Steak

MAKES 4 SERVINGS

1 medium onion, sliced

1½ pounds ground beef

1 egg

½ cup seasoned dry bread crumbs

2 teaspoons Worcestershire sauce, divided

1 teaspoon dry mustard

1 can (10½ ounces) cream of mushroom soup

½ cup water

3 tablespoons ketchup

½ cup sliced mushrooms

Chopped fresh Italian parsley (optional)

Mashed potatoes (optional)

Steamed peas (optional)

1. Spray inside of **CROCK-POT**® slow cooker with nonstick cooking spray. Layer onion in bottom of **CROCK-POT**® slow cooker.

2. Combine beef, egg, bread crumbs, 1 teaspoon Worcestershire sauce and mustard in large bowl. Form into four 1-inch-thick oval patties. Heat large nonstick skillet over medium-high heat. Add patties; cook 2 minutes per side or until lightly browned. Remove to **CROCK-POT**® slow cooker. Stir soup, water, ketchup and remaining 1 teaspoon Worcestershire sauce in medium bowl. Pour mixture over patties; top with mushrooms. Cover; cook on LOW 3 to 3½ hours. Garnish with parsley. Serve with potatoes and peas, if desired.

Slow-Cooked Chicken Fajitas

MAKES 6 SERVINGS

2 tablespoons olive oil

6 boneless, skinless chicken breasts (about 2 pounds), cut into thin strips

½ teaspoon salt

¼ teaspoon black pepper

½ medium red bell pepper, sliced

½ medium green bell pepper, sliced

½ medium yellow bell pepper, sliced

1 medium onion, sliced

¾ cup chicken broth

1 tablespoon Worcestershire sauce

2 tablespoons all-purpose flour

2 teaspoons garlic powder

1 teaspoon ground cumin

1 teaspoon dried oregano

1 teaspoon paprika

⅛ teaspoon ground red pepper

14 grape tomatoes

2 tablespoons chopped fresh cilantro

1 tablespoon lime juice

12 (6-inch) corn tortillas, warmed

Optional toppings: guacamole, sour cream, lime wedges, sprigs fresh cilantro and/or salsa

1. Heat 1 tablespoon oil in large skillet over medium-high heat. Sprinkle chicken with salt and black pepper. Add half of chicken to skillet; cook 4 to 6 minutes or until browned, turning occasionally. Remove to large paper towel-lined plate. Repeat with remaining 1 tablespoon oil and chicken.

2. Add bell peppers and onion to **CROCK-POT®** slow cooker; top with chicken. Combine broth, Worcestershire sauce, flour, garlic powder, cumin, oregano, paprika and ground red pepper in medium bowl; stir to blend. Add broth mixture to **CROCK-POT®** slow cooker.

3. Cover; cook on LOW 8 to 9 hours or on HIGH 4 to 4½ hours. Stir in tomatoes 30 minutes before end of cooking. Turn off heat. Stir in cilantro and lime juice. Serve in tortillas. Top as desired.

Southwestern Pork Chop Dinner

MAKES 6 SERVINGS

1 package (about 1 ounce) taco seasoning mix, divided

6 boneless pork chops (cut to 1-inch thickness)

1 tablespoon vegetable or olive oil

1 can (about 14 ounces) diced tomatoes, drained

1 can (about 15 ounces) pinto or kidney beans, drained

1 cup frozen corn

1 tablespoon water

1 tablespoon cornstarch

1. Rub 2 tablespoons taco seasoning mix over both sides of pork chops. Heat oil in large skillet over medium heat. Add pork chops; cook 2 minutes per side or until browned.

2. Meanwhile, combine tomatoes, beans, corn and remaining taco seasoning mix in **CROCK-POT**® slow cooker; mix well. Stack browned chops over bean mixture.

3. Cover; cook on LOW 5 to 6 hours or on HIGH 2 to 3 hours or until internal temperature of pork reaches 145°F. Remove pork to plate; cover with foil to keep warm.

4. Stir water into cornstarch in small bowl until smooth; whisk into bean mixture. Cover; cook on HIGH 10 minutes or until thickened. Serve with pork chops.

Spicy Sausage Bolognese Sauce

MAKES 6 SERVINGS

2 tablespoons olive oil, divided

1 pound ground beef

1 pound hot Italian sausage, casings removed

¼ pound pancetta, diced

1 large onion, finely diced

2 medium carrots, finely diced

1 large stalk celery, finely diced

½ teaspoon salt

½ teaspoon black pepper

3 tablespoons tomato paste

1 tablespoon minced garlic

2 cans (28 ounces *each*) diced tomatoes, drained

¾ cup whole milk

¾ cup dry red wine

1 pound hot cooked spaghetti (optional)

½ cup grated Parmesan cheese (optional)

1. Heat 1 tablespoon oil in large skillet over medium-high heat. Brown beef and sausage 6 to 8 minutes, stirring to break up meat. Drain fat. Remove to **CROCK-POT**® slow cooker. Wipe out skillet with paper towels; return to heat.

2. Add remaining 1 tablespoon oil to skillet. Add pancetta; cook until crisp and brown, stirring occasionally. Remove to **CROCK-POT**® slow cooker using slotted spoon.

3. Reduce heat to medium. Add onion, carrots, celery, salt and pepper to skillet; cook and stir 6 to 8 minutes until onion is translucent and carrots and celery are just tender. Stir in tomato paste and garlic. Cook 1 minute, stirring constantly, then add onion mixture to **CROCK-POT**® slow cooker. Stir tomatoes, milk and wine into **CROCK-POT**® slow cooker. Cover; cook on LOW 6 hours. Reserve 5 cups sauce for another use. Serve remaining 6 cups sauce with spaghetti, if desired. Sprinkle with cheese just before serving.

Braised Sea Bass with Aromatic Vegetables

MAKES 6 SERVINGS

2 tablespoons butter or olive oil

2 fennel bulbs, thinly sliced

3 large carrots, julienned

3 large leeks, cleaned and thinly sliced

Salt and black pepper

6 sea bass fillets or other firm-fleshed white fish (2 to 3 pounds *total*)

1. Melt butter in large skillet over medium-high heat. Add fennel, carrots and leeks; cook and stir 6 to 8 minutes or until beginning to soften and lightly brown. Season with salt and pepper. Arrange half of vegetables in bottom of **CROCK-POT**® slow cooker.

2. Season bass with salt and pepper; place on top of vegetables in **CROCK-POT**® slow cooker. Top with remaining vegetables. Cover; cook on LOW 2 to 3 hours or on HIGH 1 to 1½ hours or until fish begins to flake when tested with fork.

Sicilian Steak Pinwheels

MAKES 4 TO 6 SERVINGS

¾ pound mild or hot Italian sausage, casings removed

1¾ cups fresh bread crumbs

¾ cup grated Parmesan cheese

2 eggs

3 tablespoons minced fresh Italian parsley, plus additional for garnish

1½ to 2 pounds beef round steak

1 cup frozen peas

Kitchen string, cut into 15-inch lengths

1 cup pasta sauce

1 cup beef broth

1. Coat inside of **CROCK-POT**® slow cooker with nonstick cooking spray. Combine sausage, bread crumbs, cheese, eggs and 3 tablespoons parsley in large bowl until well blended; mix well.

2. Place round steak between two large sheets of plastic wrap. Using tenderizer mallet or back of skillet, pound steak until meat is about ⅜ inch thick. Remove top layer of plastic wrap. Spread sausage mixture over steak. Press frozen peas into sausage mixture. Lift edge of plastic wrap at short end; roll up steak completely. Tie at 2-inch intervals with kitchen string. Remove to **CROCK-POT**® slow cooker.

3. Combine pasta sauce and broth in medium bowl. Pour over steak. Cover; cook on LOW 6 hours.

4. Turn off heat. Remove steak to large serving platter. Cover loosely with foil 10 to 15 minutes before removing string and slicing. Let cooking liquid stand 5 minutes. Skim off fat and discard. Serve steak with cooking liquid.

Sweet and Sour Chicken

MAKES 4 SERVINGS

1 pound boneless, skinless chicken thighs, cut into 1-inch pieces

¼ cup chicken broth

2 tablespoons soy sauce

2 tablespoons hoisin sauce

1 tablespoon cider vinegar

1 tablespoon tomato paste

2 teaspoons packed brown sugar

1 clove garlic, minced

¼ teaspoon black pepper

2 teaspoons cornstarch

2 tablespoons snipped fresh chives

Hot cooked rice

1. Combine chicken, broth, soy sauce, hoisin sauce, vinegar, tomato paste, brown sugar, garlic and pepper in **CROCK-POT**® slow cooker; stir to blend. Cover; cook on LOW 2½ to 3½ hours.

2. Remove chicken to large cutting board using slotted spoon. Cover loosely with foil to keep warm. Stir 2 tablespoons cooking liquid into cornstarch in small bowl until smooth; whisk into **CROCK-POT**® slow cooker. Stir in chives. Turn **CROCK-POT**® slow cooker to HIGH. Cover; cook on HIGH 10 to 15 minutes or until sauce is slightly thickened. Serve chicken and sauce over rice.

Turkey Breast with Sweet Cranberry Sauce

MAKES 8 SERVINGS

1 fresh or thawed bone-in turkey breast (6 to 7 pounds), rinsed and patted dry*

1 can (16 ounces) whole berry cranberry sauce

1 packet (1 ounce) dry onion soup mix

Grated peel and juice of 1 orange

3 tablespoons soy sauce

2 to 3 tablespoons cornstarch

1 tablespoon sugar

1 teaspoon cider vinegar

Salt

Substitute two 3½-pound bone-in turkey breast halves, if necessary.

1. Coat inside of **CROCK-POT**® slow cooker with nonstick cooking spray. Place turkey in bottom, meat side up. Combine cranberry sauce, dry soup mix, orange peel and orange juice in medium bowl. Pour over turkey. Cover; cook on HIGH 3½ hours.

2. Scoop cranberry mixture off of turkey into cooking liquid. Remove turkey to large cutting board. Cover loosely with foil; let stand 15 minutes before slicing.

3. Stir soy sauce into cornstarch in small bowl until smooth; whisk into cooking liquid with sugar, vinegar and salt. Cover; cook on HIGH 15 minutes or until thickened slightly. Serve sauce over sliced turkey.

Portuguese Madeira Beef Shanks

MAKES 4 SERVINGS

1 large white onion, diced

1 green bell pepper, diced

½ cup diced celery

½ cup minced fresh Italian parsley

2 jalapeño peppers, seeded and minced*

4 cloves garlic, minced

4 medium beef shanks, bone-in (about 3 pounds *total*)

1 tablespoon fresh rosemary, minced

1 teaspoon salt

1 cup beef broth

1 cup dry Madeira wine

4 cups hot cooked rice

Horseradish sauce (optional)

*Jalapeño peppers can sting and irritate the skin, so wear rubber gloves when handling peppers and do not touch your eyes.

1. Place onion, bell pepper, celery, parsley, jalapeño peppers and garlic in **CROCK-POT**® slow cooker.

2. Rub beef shanks with rosemary and salt. Place shanks on top of vegetables. Pour broth and wine over shanks and vegetables. Cover; cook on LOW 7 to 9 hours.

3. To serve, spoon 1 cup rice into each soup bowl. Top rice with beef shank. Spoon vegetable sauce over shanks. Serve with horseradish sauce, if desired.

New England Chuck Roast

MAKES 8 SERVINGS

1 boneless beef chuck roast
(4 to 5 pounds), string on*

2 teaspoons salt

¼ teaspoon black pepper
Olive oil

4 cups water, divided

2 cups carrots, cut into 2-inch
pieces

1½ cups yellow onion, cut into
quarters

4 small red potatoes, cut into
quarters

2 stalks celery, cut into 1-inch
pieces

3 whole bay leaves

2 tablespoons white vinegar

2 tablespoons prepared
horseradish

1 head cabbage, cut into
quarters or eighths

4 tablespoons all-purpose flour

2 tablespoons cornstarch

*Unless you have a 5-, 6- or 7-quart
CROCK-POT® slow cooker, cut any
roast larger than 2½ pounds in half so
it cooks completely.*

1. Season roast with salt and pepper. Heat oil in large skillet over medium heat. Brown roast on all sides. Remove to **CROCK-POT**® slow cooker.

2. Add 3 cups water, carrots, onion, potatoes, celery, bay leaves, vinegar and horseradish. Cover; cook on LOW 5 to 7 hours or on HIGH 2 to 4 hours.

3. One hour before serving, add cabbage to **CROCK-POT**® slow cooker. Stir remaining 1 cup water into flour and cornstarch in medium bowl until smooth; whisk flour mixture into **CROCK-POT**® slow cooker. Cover; cook on HIGH 1 hour or until thickened. Remove and discard bay leaves. Remove roast to large cutting board. Cover loosely with foil; let stand 10 to 15 minutes. Remove and discard string. Slice roast; serve with sauce and vegetables.

Turkey Tacos

MAKES 4 SERVINGS

- 1 pound ground turkey
- 1 medium onion, chopped
- 1 can (6 ounces) tomato paste
- ½ cup chunky salsa
- 1 tablespoon chopped fresh cilantro
- ½ teaspoon salt

- 1 tablespoon butter
- 1 tablespoon all-purpose flour
- ¼ teaspoon salt
- ⅓ cup milk
- ½ cup sour cream
- Pinch ground red pepper
- 8 taco shells

1. Brown turkey and onion in large skillet over medium heat, stirring to break up meat. Combine turkey mixture, tomato paste, salsa, cilantro and salt in **CROCK-POT**® slow cooker. Cover; cook on LOW 4 to 5 hours.

2. Just before serving, melt butter in small saucepan over low heat. Whisk in flour and salt; cook 1 minute. Whisk in milk; cook and stir over low heat until thickened. Remove from heat. Combine sour cream and ground red pepper in small bowl. Stir into hot milk mixture. Cook over low heat 1 minute, stirring constantly.

3. Spoon ¼ cup turkey mixture into each taco shell; top with sauce.

> TIP: When adapting recipes for your **CROCK-POT**® slow cooker, adjust the amount of herbs and spices. Whole herbs and spices increase in flavor while ground spices tend to lose flavor during slow cooking. If you prefer, you can adjust the seasonings or add herbs and spices just before serving.

Molasses Maple-Glazed Beef Brisket

MAKES 4 TO 6 SERVINGS

- 1 beef brisket (1½ to 2 pounds), scored on both sides
- 4 slices (⅟₁₆ inch thick *each*) fresh ginger
- 4 slices (1½×½ inches *each*) orange peel
- ½ cup maple syrup
- ¼ cup molasses
- Juice of 1 orange
- 2 tablespoons packed light brown sugar
- 2 tablespoons olive oil
- 1 tablespoon tomato paste
- 2 cloves garlic, crushed
- 1 tablespoon salt
- 1 teaspoon ground red pepper
- ½ teaspoon black pepper
- Hot mashed potatoes (optional)
- Green beans (optional)

1. Combine brisket, ginger, orange peel, syrup, molasses, orange juice, brown sugar, oil, tomato paste, garlic, salt, ground red pepper and black pepper in large resealable food storage bag. Seal bag; turn to coat. Refrigerate 2 hours or overnight, turning bag several times.

2. Remove brisket to **CROCK-POT**® slow cooker. Cover; cook on LOW 7 to 9 hours or on HIGH 3½ to 4 hours. Remove brisket to large cutting board; thinly slice across grain. Serve with potatoes and green beans, if desired.

Slow Cooker Pizza Casserole

MAKES 6 SERVINGS

1½ pounds ground beef

1 pound bulk pork sausage

4 jars (14 ounces *each*) pizza sauce

2 cups (8 ounces) shredded mozzarella cheese

2 cups grated Parmesan cheese

2 cans (4 ounces *each*) mushroom stems and pieces, drained

2 packages (3 ounces *each*) sliced pepperoni

½ cup finely chopped onion

½ cup finely chopped green bell pepper

1 clove garlic, minced

1 pound corkscrew pasta, cooked and drained

1. Brown beef and sausage in large nonstick skillet over medium-high heat 6 to 8 minutes, stirring to break up meat. Remove beef mixture to **CROCK-POT**® slow cooker using slotted spoon.

2. Add pizza sauce, cheeses, mushrooms, pepperoni, onion, bell pepper and garlic; stir to blend. Cover; cook on LOW 3½ hours or on HIGH 2 hours.

3. Stir in pasta. Cover; cook on HIGH 15 to 20 minutes or until pasta is heated through.

Sides

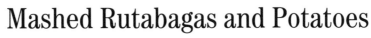

Mashed Rutabagas and Potatoes

MAKES 8 SERVINGS

2 pounds rutabagas, peeled and cut into ½-inch pieces

1 pound potatoes, peeled and cut into ½-inch pieces

½ cup milk

½ teaspoon ground nutmeg

2 tablespoons chopped fresh Italian parsley

Sprigs fresh Italian parsley (optional)

1. Place rutabagas and potatoes in **CROCK-POT**® slow cooker; add enough water to cover vegetables. Cover; cook on LOW 6 hours or on HIGH 3 hours. Remove vegetables to large bowl using slotted spoon. Discard cooking liquid.

2. Mash vegetables with potato masher. Add milk, nutmeg and chopped parsley; stir until smooth. Garnish with parsley sprigs.

White Beans and Tomatoes

MAKES 8 TO 10 SERVINGS

¼ cup olive oil
2 medium onions, chopped
1 tablespoon minced garlic
4 cups water
2 cans (about 14 ounces *each*) cannellini beans
1 can (about 28 ounces) crushed tomatoes

4 teaspoons dried oregano
2 teaspoons kosher salt
  Black pepper (optional)
  Sprigs fresh oregano (optional)

1. Heat oil in large skillet over medium heat. Add onions; cook 15 minutes or until tender and translucent, stirring occasionally. Add garlic; cook 1 minute.

2. Remove mixture to **CROCK-POT**® slow cooker. Add water, beans, tomatoes, dried oregano and salt. Cover; cook on LOW 8 hours or on HIGH 4 hours. Stir in pepper, if desired. Garnish with fresh oregano.

Buttermilk Corn Bread

MAKES 1 LOAF

1½ cups cornmeal
½ cup all-purpose flour
1 tablespoon sugar
2 teaspoons baking powder
½ teaspoon salt
1½ cups buttermilk
½ teaspoon baking soda
2 eggs
¼ cup (½ stick) butter, melted

¼ cup chopped seeded jalapeño peppers*
1 tablespoon finely chopped pimientos or roasted red pepper

*Jalapeño peppers can sting and irritate the skin, so wear rubber gloves when handling peppers and do not touch your eyes.

1. Coat inside of **CROCK-POT®** slow cooker with nonstick cooking spray.

2. Sift cornmeal, flour, sugar, baking powder and salt into large bowl. Whisk buttermilk into baking soda in medium bowl. Add eggs to buttermilk mixture; whisk lightly until blended. Stir in butter.

3. Stir buttermilk mixture, jalapeño peppers and pimientos into cornmeal mixture until just blended. *Do not overmix.* Pour into **CROCK-POT®** slow cooker. Cover; cook on HIGH 1½ to 2 hours.

Collard Greens

MAKES 10 SERVINGS

4 bunches collard greens, stemmed, washed and torn into bite-size pieces

2 cups water

½ medium red bell pepper, cut into strips

⅓ medium green bell pepper, cut into strips

¼ cup olive oil

¼ teaspoon salt

¼ teaspoon black pepper

Combine collard greens, water, bell peppers, oil, salt and black pepper in **CROCK-POT**® slow cooker. Cover; cook on LOW 3 to 4 hours or on HIGH 2 hours.

Braised Beets with Cranberries

MAKES 6 TO 8 SERVINGS

2½ pounds medium beets,
    peeled and cut into
    wedges

1 cup cranberry juice

½ cup sweetened dried
    cranberries

2 tablespoons quick-cooking
    tapioca

2 tablespoons butter, cubed

2 tablespoons honey

½ teaspoon salt

⅓ cup crumbled blue cheese
    (optional)

Orange peel, thinly sliced
    (optional)

1. Combine beets, cranberry juice, cranberries, tapioca, butter, honey and salt in **CROCK-POT**® slow cooker; stir to blend. Cover; cook on LOW 7 to 8 hours.

2. Remove beets to large serving bowl using slotted spoon. Pour half of cooking liquid over beets. Garnish with blue cheese and orange peel.

Colcannon

MAKES 8 SERVINGS

6 tablespoons butter, cut into small pieces

3 pounds russet potatoes, peeled and cut into 1-inch pieces

2 medium leeks (white and light green parts only), thinly sliced

½ cup water

2½ teaspoons kosher salt

¼ teaspoon black pepper

1 cup milk

½ small head (about 1 pound) savoy cabbage, cored and thinly sliced

4 slices bacon, crisp-cooked and crumbled

1. Sprinkle butter in bottom of **CROCK-POT**® slow cooker. Layer half of potatoes, leeks, remaining potatoes, water, salt and pepper. Cover; cook on HIGH 5 hours or until potatoes are tender, stirring halfway through cooking time.

2. Mash potatoes in **CROCK-POT**® slow cooker until smooth. Stir in milk and cabbage. Cover; cook on HIGH 30 to 40 minutes or until cabbage is crisp-tender. Stir bacon into potato mixture.

Spinach Gorgonzola Corn Bread

MAKES 1 LOAF

2 boxes (8½ ounces *each*) corn bread mix

1 package (10 ounces) frozen chopped spinach, thawed and drained

1 cup crumbled Gorgonzola cheese

3 eggs

½ cup whipping cream

1 teaspoon black pepper

Paprika (optional)

1. Coat inside of 5-quart **CROCK-POT®** slow cooker with nonstick cooking spray. Combine corn bread mix, spinach, cheese, eggs, cream, pepper and paprika, if desired, in medium bowl; stir to blend. Place batter in **CROCK-POT®** slow cooker.

2. Cover; cook on HIGH 1½ hours. Turn off heat. Let bread cool completely before inverting onto large serving platter.

NOTE: Cook only on HIGH setting for proper crust and texture.

Curried Lentils with Fruit

5 cups water

1½ cups dried brown lentils, rinsed and sorted

1 Granny Smith apple, chopped, plus additional for garnish

¼ cup golden raisins

¼ cup lemon nonfat yogurt

1 teaspoon salt

1 teaspoon curry powder

1. Combine water, lentils, 1 apple and raisins in **CROCK-POT**® slow cooker. Cover; cook on LOW 8 to 9 hours or until lentils are tender. (Lentils should absorb most or all of the water. Slightly tilt **CROCK-POT**® slow cooker to check.)

2. Remove lentil mixture to large bowl; stir in yogurt, salt and curry powder until blended. Garnish with additional apple.

Confetti Black Beans

MAKES 6 SERVINGS

1 cup dried black beans, rinsed and sorted

1½ teaspoons olive oil

1 medium onion, chopped

¼ cup chopped red bell pepper

¼ cup chopped yellow bell pepper

1 jalapeño pepper, finely chopped*

1 large tomato, chopped

½ teaspoon salt

⅛ teaspoon black pepper

2 cloves garlic, minced

1 can (about 14 ounces) chicken broth

1 whole bay leaf

Hot pepper sauce (optional)

Jalapeño peppers can sting and irritate the skin, so wear rubber gloves when handling peppers and do not touch your eyes.

1. Place beans in large bowl and add enough cold water to cover by at least 2 inches. Soak 6 to 8 hours or overnight.** Drain beans; discard water.

2. Heat oil in large skillet over medium heat. Add onion, bell peppers and jalapeño pepper; cook and stir 5 minutes or until onion is tender. Add tomato, salt and black pepper; cook 5 minutes. Stir in garlic.

3. Place beans, broth and bay leaf in **CROCK-POT**® slow cooker. Add onion mixture. Cover; cook on LOW 7 to 8 hours or on HIGH 4½ to 5 hours. Remove and discard bay leaf. Serve with hot pepper sauce, if desired.

**To quick soak beans, place beans in large saucepan; cover with water. Bring to a boil over high heat. Boil 2 minutes. Remove from heat; let soak, covered, 1 hour.

Fennel Braised with Tomato

MAKES 6 SERVINGS

2 fennel bulbs
1 tablespoon olive oil
1 onion, sliced
1 clove garlic, sliced
4 tomatoes, chopped
⅔ cup vegetable broth

3 tablespoons dry white wine
1 tablespoon chopped fresh marjoram *or* 1 teaspoon dried marjoram
Salt and black pepper

1. Trim stems and bottoms from fennel bulbs, reserving green leafy tops for garnish. Cut each bulb lengthwise into four wedges.

2. Heat oil in large skillet over medium heat. Add fennel, onion and garlic; cook and stir 5 minutes or until onion is soft and translucent. Remove fennel mixture to **CROCK-POT**® slow cooker. Add tomatoes, broth, wine, marjoram, salt and pepper; stir to blend.

3. Cover; cook on LOW 2 to 3 hours or on HIGH 1 to 1½ hours. Garnish with reserved green leafy tops.

French Carrot Medley

MAKES 6 SERVINGS

2 cups sliced carrots
¾ cup orange juice
1 can (4 ounces) sliced
   mushrooms, undrained
4 stalks celery, sliced
2 tablespoons chopped onion

½ teaspoon dried dill weed
   Salt and black pepper
¼ cup cold water
2 teaspoons cornstarch

1. Combine carrots, orange juice, mushrooms, celery, onion, dill weed, salt and pepper in **CROCK-POT**® slow cooker. Cover; cook on LOW 3 to 4 hours or on HIGH 2 hours.

2. Stir water into cornstarch in small bowl until smooth; whisk into cooking liquid. Cover; cook on HIGH 15 minutes or until sauce is thickened. Spoon sauce over vegetable mixture before serving.

Focaccia with Rosemary and Romano

MAKES 8 TO 10 SERVINGS

1¼ cups warm water (100° to 110°F)

1 package (¼ ounce) active dry yeast

1 tablespoon sugar

3 to 3½ cups all-purpose flour, plus additional for work surface

1½ tablespoons finely chopped fresh rosemary

2 teaspoons salt

½ teaspoon red pepper flakes

3 tablespoons extra virgin olive oil

¼ cup grated Romano cheese

1. Coat inside of **CROCK-POT**® slow cooker with nonstick cooking spray. Combine water, yeast and sugar in small bowl; let stand 5 minutes until frothy. Combine flour, rosemary, salt and red pepper flakes in large bowl; stir to blend. Pour water mixture and oil into flour mixture; stir until soft dough forms. Turn dough out onto lightly floured surface; knead 5 minutes. Place dough in **CROCK-POT**® slow cooker; stretch to fit bottom. Cover; let stand 1 hour in warm place (85°F) until doubled in size.

2. Gently press dough with fingertips to deflate. Sprinkle with cheese. Cover; let rise 30 minutes. Place clean, dry towel over top of **CROCK-POT**® slow cooker; then replace the lid. Cover; cook on HIGH 2 hours or until dough is lightly browned on sides. Remove to wire rack. Let stand 10 to 15 minutes before slicing.

Garlicky Mustard Greens

MAKES 4 SERVINGS

2 pounds mustard greens
1 teaspoon olive oil
1 cup chopped onion
2 cloves garlic, minced
¾ cup chopped red bell pepper

½ cup chicken or vegetable broth
1 tablespoon cider vinegar
1 teaspoon sugar

1. Remove stems and any wilted leaves from greens. Stack several leaves; roll up. Cut crosswise into 1-inch slices. Repeat with remaining greens.

2. Heat oil in large saucepan over medium heat. Add onion and garlic; cook and stir 5 minutes or until onion is tender. Combine greens, onion mixture, bell pepper and broth in **CROCK-POT**® slow cooker; stir to blend. Cover; cook on LOW 3 to 4 hours or on HIGH 2 hours.

3. Combine vinegar and sugar in small bowl; stir until sugar is dissolved. Stir into cooked greens; serve immediately.

Frijoles Borrachos (Drunken Beans)

MAKES 8 SERVINGS

6 slices bacon, chopped

1 medium yellow onion, chopped

1 tablespoon minced garlic

3 jalapeño peppers, seeded and finely diced*

1 tablespoon dried oregano

1 can (12 ounces) beer

6 cups water

1 pound dried pinto beans, rinsed and sorted

1 can (about 14 ounces) diced tomatoes

1 tablespoon kosher salt

¼ cup chopped fresh cilantro

*Jalapeño peppers can sting and irritate the skin, so wear rubber gloves when handling peppers and do not touch your eyes.

1. Heat large skillet over medium-high heat. Add bacon; cook 5 minutes or until mostly browned and crisp. Remove to **CROCK-POT**® slow cooker using slotted spoon. Discard all but 3 tablespoons of drippings.

2. Heat same skillet over medium heat. Add onion; cook 6 minutes or until softened and lightly browned. Add garlic, jalapeño peppers and oregano; cook 30 seconds or until fragrant. Increase heat to medium-high. Add beer; bring to a simmer. Cook 2 minutes, stirring and scraping up any brown bits from bottom of skillet. Remove mixture to **CROCK-POT**® slow cooker.

3. Add water, beans, tomatoes and salt to **CROCK-POT**® slow cooker. Cover; cook on LOW 7 hours or on HIGH 3 to 4 hours or until beans are tender. Mash beans slightly until broth is thickened and creamy. Top with cilantro.

Lemon Cauliflower

MAKES 6 SERVINGS

1 tablespoon butter

3 cloves garlic, minced

2 tablespoons lemon juice

½ cup water

4 tablespoons chopped fresh Italian parsley, divided

½ teaspoon grated lemon peel

6 cups (about 1½ pounds) cauliflower florets

¼ cup grated Parmesan cheese (optional)

Lemon slices (optional)

1. Heat butter in small saucepan over medium heat. Add garlic; cook and stir 2 to 3 minutes or until soft. Stir in lemon juice and water.

2. Combine garlic mixture, 1 tablespoon parsley, lemon peel and cauliflower in **CROCK-POT**® slow cooker; stir to blend. Cover; cook on LOW 4 hours.

3. Sprinkle with remaining 3 tablespoons parsley and cheese, if desired, before serving. Garnish with lemon slices.

Curried Potatoes, Cauliflower and Peas

MAKES 6 SERVINGS

1 tablespoon vegetable oil

1 large yellow onion, chopped

2 tablespoons peeled and minced fresh ginger

2 cloves garlic, chopped

2 pounds red potatoes, cut into ½-inch-thick rounds

1 teaspoon garam masala*

2 teaspoons salt

1 small head cauliflower (about 1¼ pounds), trimmed and broken into florets

1 cup vegetable broth

2 plum tomatoes, seeded and chopped

1 cup frozen peas, thawed

Hot cooked basmati or long grain rice (optional)

Garam masala is an Indian spice blend available in the spice aisle of many supermarkets. If garam masala is unavailable substitute ½ teaspoon ground cumin and ½ teaspoon ground coriander seeds.

1. Heat oil in large skillet over medium heat. Add onion, ginger and garlic; cook and stir 3 to 5 minutes or until onion is tender. Remove from heat.

2. Place potatoes in **CROCK-POT®** slow cooker. Mix garam masala and salt in small bowl. Sprinkle half of spice mixture over potatoes. Top with onion mixture, then cauliflower. Sprinkle remaining spice mixture over cauliflower. Pour in broth. Cover; cook on HIGH 3½ hours.

3. Stir in tomatoes and peas. Cover; cook on HIGH 30 minutes or until potatoes are tender. Serve over rice, if desired.

Brussels Sprouts with Bacon, Thyme and Raisins

MAKES 8 SERVINGS

2 pounds Brussels sprouts, ends trimmed and cut in half lengthwise

1 cup chicken broth

⅔ cup golden raisins

2 thick slices applewood smoked bacon, chopped

2 tablespoons chopped fresh thyme

Combine sprouts, broth, raisins, bacon and thyme in **CROCK-POT**® slow cooker; stir to blend. Cover; cook on LOW 3 to 4 hours.

Corn Bread Stuffing with Sausage and Green Apples

MAKES 8 TO 12 SERVINGS

1 package (16 ounces) honey corn bread mix, plus ingredients to prepare mix

2 cups cubed French bread

1½ pounds mild Italian sausage, casings removed

1 onion, finely chopped

1 green apple, peeled, cored and diced

2 stalks celery, finely chopped

½ teaspoon salt

¼ teaspoon dried sage

¼ teaspoon dried rosemary

¼ teaspoon dried thyme

¼ teaspoon black pepper

3 cups chicken broth

2 tablespoons chopped fresh Italian parsley (optional)

1. Mix and bake corn bread according to package directions. When cool, cover with plastic wrap and set aside overnight.*

2. Coat inside of **CROCK-POT®** slow cooker with nonstick cooking spray. Preheat oven to 350°F. Cut corn bread into 1-inch cubes. Spread corn bread and French bread on baking sheet. Toast in oven 20 minutes or until dry.

3. Brown sausage in medium skillet over medium heat 6 to 8 minutes, stirring to break up meat. Drain fat. Remove sausage to **CROCK-POT®** slow cooker using slotted spoon.

4. Add onion, apple and celery to skillet; cook and stir 5 minutes or until softened. Stir in salt, sage, rosemary, thyme and pepper. Remove mixture to **CROCK-POT®** slow cooker.

5. Add bread cubes; stir gently to combine. Pour broth over mixture. Cover; cook on HIGH 3 to 3½ hours or until liquid is absorbed. Garnish with parsley.

*Or purchase prepared 8-inch square pan of corn bread. Proceed as directed.

TIP: Consider using your **CROCK-POT**® slow cooker as an extra "oven" or "burner" for entertaining. For example, the **CROCK-POT**® slow cooker can cook the stuffing while the holiday turkey is in the oven.

Lemon and Tangerine Glazed Carrots

MAKES 10 TO 12 SERVINGS

6 cups sliced carrots
1½ cups apple juice
6 tablespoons butter
¼ cup packed brown sugar
2 tablespoons grated lemon peel

2 tablespoons grated tangerine peel
½ teaspoon salt
Chopped fresh Italian parsley (optional)

Combine carrots, apple juice, butter, brown sugar, lemon peel, tangerine peel and salt in **CROCK-POT®** slow cooker; stir to blend. Cover; cook on LOW 4 to 5 hours or on HIGH 1 to 3 hours. Garnish with parsley.

Lemon Dilled Parsnips and Turnips

MAKES 8 TO 10 SERVINGS

4 turnips, peeled and cut into ½-inch pieces

3 parsnips, cut into ½-inch pieces

2 cups chicken broth

¼ cup chopped green onions

¼ cup lemon juice

¼ cup dried dill weed

1 teaspoon minced garlic

¼ cup cold water

¼ cup cornstarch

1. Combine turnips, parsnips, broth, green onions, lemon juice, dill weed and garlic in **CROCK-POT**® slow cooker. Cover; cook on LOW 3 to 4 hours or on HIGH 1 to 3 hours.

2. Stir water into cornstarch in small bowl until smooth; whisk into **CROCK-POT**® slow cooker. Cover; cook on HIGH 15 minutes or until thickened.

Rustic Cheddar Mashed Potatoes

MAKES 8 SERVINGS

2 pounds russet potatoes, diced

1 cup water

2 tablespoons butter, cubed

¾ cup milk

Salt and black pepper

¾ cup (3 ounces) shredded Cheddar cheese

½ cup finely chopped green onions

1. Combine potatoes, water and butter in **CROCK-POT®** slow cooker. Cover; cook on LOW 6 hours or on HIGH 3 hours. Remove potatoes to large bowl using slotted spoon.

2. Beat potatoes with electric mixer at medium speed 2 to 3 minutes or until well blended. Add milk, salt and pepper; beat 2 minutes or until well blended.

3. Stir in cheese and green onions. Turn off heat. Cover; let stand 15 minutes or until cheese is melted.

Orange-Spiced Sweet Potatoes

MAKES 8 SERVINGS

2 pounds sweet potatoes, diced

½ cup packed dark brown sugar

½ cup (1 stick) butter, cubed

1 teaspoon ground cinnamon

1 teaspoon vanilla

½ teaspoon salt

½ teaspoon ground nutmeg

½ teaspoon grated orange peel

Juice of 1 medium orange

Chopped toasted pecans*

*To toast pecans, spread in a single layer in small skillet. Cook and stir over medium heat 1 to 2 minutes or until nuts are lightly browned.

Combine potatoes, brown sugar, butter, cinnamon, vanilla, salt, nutmeg, orange peel and juice in **CROCK-POT**® slow cooker; stir to blend. Cover; cook on LOW 4 hours or on HIGH 2 hours. Sprinkle with pecans.

VARIATION: For creamier potatoes, beat ¼ cup milk or whipping cream into potatoes. Beat with electric mixer at medium speed until smooth. Sprinkle with pecans.

Cheesy Mashed Potato Casserole

MAKES 10 TO 12 SERVINGS

4 pounds Yukon Gold potatoes, peeled and cut into 1-inch pieces
2 cups vegetable broth
3 tablespoons unsalted butter, cubed
½ cup milk, heated
⅓ cup sour cream

2 cups (8 ounces) shredded sharp Cheddar cheese, plus additional for garnish
½ teaspoon salt
¼ teaspoon black pepper
Chopped fresh Italian parsley (optional)

1. Coat inside of **CROCK-POT®** slow cooker with nonstick cooking spray. Add potatoes and broth; dot with butter. Cover; cook on LOW 4½ to 5 hours.

2. Mash potatoes with potato masher; stir in milk, sour cream, 2 cups cheese, salt and pepper until cheese is melted. Garnish with additional cheese and parsley.

BBQ Baked Beans

MAKES 12 SERVINGS

3 cans (about 15 ounces *each*)
  white beans, drained
4 slices bacon, chopped

¾ cup prepared barbecue sauce
½ cup maple syrup
1½ teaspoons dry mustard

Coat inside of **CROCK-POT**® slow cooker with nonstick cooking spray. Add beans, bacon, barbecue sauce, syrup and mustard; stir to blend. Cover; cook on LOW 4 hours, stirring halfway through cooking time.

Desserts

Spiced Apple and Cranberry Compote

MAKES 6 SERVINGS

2½ cups cranberry juice cocktail

1 package (6 ounces) dried apples

½ cup (2 ounces) dried cranberries

½ cup Rhine wine or apple juice

½ cup honey

2 whole cinnamon sticks, broken into halves

Ice cream (optional)

1. Combine juice, apples, cranberries, wine, honey and cinnamon stick halves in **CROCK-POT®** slow cooker; stir to blend. Cover; cook on LOW 4 to 5 hours or until liquid is absorbed and fruit is tender.

2. Remove and discard cinnamon sticks. Serve with ice cream, if desired.

5-Ingredient Kheer

MAKES 6 TO 8 SERVINGS

4 cups whole milk

¾ cup sugar

1 cup uncooked white basmati
rice, rinsed and drained

½ cup golden raisins

3 whole green cardamom
pods *or* ¼ teaspoon ground
cardamom

Coat inside of **CROCK-POT**® slow cooker with nonstick cooking spray. Add milk and sugar; stir until sugar is dissolved. Add rice, raisins and cardamom. Cover; cook on HIGH 1 hour. Stir. Cover; cook on HIGH 1½ to 2 hours or until milk has been absorbed.

Brownie Bottoms

MAKES 6 SERVINGS

½ cup packed brown sugar

½ cup water

2 tablespoons unsweetened cocoa powder

2½ cups packaged brownie mix

1 package (2¾ ounces) instant chocolate pudding mix

½ cup milk chocolate chips

2 eggs, beaten

3 tablespoons butter, melted

Whipped cream or ice cream (optional)

1. Coat inside of **CROCK-POT**® slow cooker with nonstick cooking spray. Combine brown sugar, water and cocoa in small saucepan over medium heat; bring to a boil over medium-high heat.

2. Meanwhile, combine brownie mix, pudding mix, chocolate chips, eggs and butter in medium bowl; stir until well blended. Spread batter in **CROCK-POT**® slow cooker; pour boiling sugar mixture over batter.

3. Cover; cook on HIGH 1½ hours. Turn off heat. Let stand 30 minutes. Serve with whipped cream, if desired.

NOTE: Recipe can be doubled for a 5-, 6- or 7-quart **CROCK-POT**® slow cooker.

Fruit and Nut Baked Apples

MAKES 4 SERVINGS

4 large baking apples, such as Rome Beauty or Jonathan

1 tablespoon lemon juice

⅓ cup chopped dried apricots

⅓ cup chopped walnuts or pecans

3 tablespoons packed brown sugar

½ teaspoon ground cinnamon

2 tablespoons unsalted butter, melted

½ cup water

Caramel ice cream topping (optional)

1. Scoop out center of each apple, leaving 1½-inch-wide cavity about ½ inch from bottom. Peel top of apple down about 1 inch. Brush peeled edges evenly with lemon juice. Combine apricots, walnuts, brown sugar and cinnamon in small bowl; stir to blend. Add butter; mix well. Spoon mixture evenly into apple cavities.

2. Pour water in bottom of **CROCK-POT®** slow cooker. Place 2 apples in bottom of **CROCK-POT®** slow cooker. Arrange remaining 2 apples above but not directly on top of bottom apples. Cover; cook on LOW 3 to 4 hours or until apples are tender. Serve warm or at room temperature with caramel ice cream topping, if desired.

TIP: Ever wonder why you need to brush lemon juice around the top of an apple? Citrus fruits, like lemons, contain an acid that keeps apples, potatoes and other white vegetables from discoloring once they are cut or peeled.

Strawberry Rhubarb Crisp

MAKES 8 SERVINGS

4 cups sliced hulled fresh strawberries

4 cups diced rhubarb (about 5 stalks), cut into ½-inch dice

2 cups granulated sugar, divided

2 tablespoons lemon juice

1½ tablespoons cornstarch, plus water (optional)

1 cup all-purpose flour

1 cup old-fashioned oats

½ cup packed brown sugar

½ teaspoon ground ginger

½ teaspoon ground nutmeg

½ cup (1 stick) butter, cubed

½ cup sliced almonds, toasted*

To toast almonds, spread in single layer in heavy skillet. Cook over medium heat 1 to 2 minutes or until nuts are lightly browned, stirring frequently.

1. Coat inside of **CROCK-POT**® slow cooker with nonstick cooking spray. Place strawberries, rhubarb, 1½ cups granulated sugar and lemon juice in **CROCK-POT**® slow cooker; mix well. Cover; cook on HIGH 1½ hours or until fruit is tender.

2. If fruit is dry after cooking, add a little water. If fruit has too much liquid, mix cornstarch with a little water in small bowl; whisk into liquid. Cover; cook on HIGH 15 minutes or until cooking liquid is thickened.

3. Preheat oven to 375°F. Combine flour, oats, ½ cup granulated sugar, brown sugar, ginger and nutmeg in medium bowl. Cut in butter using pastry blender or two knives until mixture resembles coarse crumbs. Stir in almonds.

4. Remove lid from **CROCK-POT**® slow cooker and gently sprinkle topping onto fruit. Remove stoneware to oven. Bake 15 to 20 minutes or until topping begins to brown.

Orange Cranberry Nut Bread

MAKES 10 SERVINGS

2 cups all-purpose flour
½ cup chopped pecans
1 teaspoon baking powder
½ teaspoon baking soda
¼ teaspoon salt
1 cup dried cranberries

2 teaspoons dried orange peel
⅔ cup boiling water
¾ cup sugar
2 tablespoons shortening
1 egg, lightly beaten
1 teaspoon vanilla

1. Coat inside of 3-quart **CROCK-POT®** slow cooker with nonstick cooking spray. Combine flour, pecans, baking powder, baking soda and salt in medium bowl.

2. Combine cranberries and orange peel in separate medium bowl; stir in boiling water. Add sugar, shortening, egg and vanilla; stir just until blended. Add flour mixture; stir just until blended.

3. Pour batter into **CROCK-POT®** slow cooker. Cover; cook on HIGH 1¼ to 1½ hours or until edges begin to brown and toothpick inserted into center comes out clean.

4. Remove stoneware insert from **CROCK-POT®** slow cooker. Cool on wire rack 10 minutes. Remove bread from insert; cool completely on rack.

TIP: This recipe works best in round **CROCK-POT®** slow cookers.

NOTE: Not all **CROCK-POT®** slow cookers have removable stoneware. For those that don't, use a prepared casserole, soufflé dish or other high-sided baking dish that fits inside the **CROCK-POT®** slow cooker.

Plum Bread Pudding

MAKES 12 TO 16 SERVINGS

1 loaf (1 pound) sliced egg bread, lightly toasted*

2 tablespoons unsalted butter, divided

12 large unpeeled Italian plums, pitted and cut into wedges (about 4 cups *total*), divided

1½ cups plus 2 tablespoons sugar, divided

3 cups half-and-half

10 eggs

1¼ cups milk

2 teaspoons vanilla

¾ teaspoon salt

¾ teaspoon ground cinnamon

Sweetened whipped cream or vanilla ice cream (optional)

Use an egg-rich bread, such as challah, for best results. For a more delicate bread pudding, substitute cinnamon rolls or plain Danish rolls.

1. Coat inside of 6-quart **CROCK-POT®** slow cooker with nonstick cooking spray. Cut toasted bread into 1-inch cubes; set aside.

2. Melt 1 tablespoon butter in large skillet over medium-high heat. Add half of sliced plums and 1 tablespoon sugar; cook 2 minutes or until plums are pulpy and release their juices. Pour plums and juices into medium bowl; repeat with remaining 1 tablespoon butter, remaining plums and 1 tablespoon sugar. Set aside.

3. Beat together half-and-half, eggs, remaining 1½ cups sugar, milk, vanilla, salt and cinnamon in large bowl. Stir in bread, plums and any accumulated juices. Spoon into **CROCK-POT®** slow cooker. Cover; cook on HIGH 3 hours or until pudding is firm when gently shaken and thin knife inserted halfway between center and edge comes out clean. Remove stoneware from base; cool 15 minutes. Serve with whipped cream, if desired.

PEACH BREAD PUDDING: If fresh plums are not available, substitute 9 large peaches, peeled, pitted and cut into wedges or 4 cups frozen sliced peaches, thawed (juices reserved).

Cherry Flan

MAKES 6 SERVINGS

5 eggs
½ cup sugar
½ teaspoon salt
¾ cup all-purpose flour
1 can (12 ounces) evaporated milk

1 teaspoon vanilla
1 bag (16 ounces) frozen pitted dark sweet cherries, thawed
Whipped cream (optional)
Fresh cherries (optional)
Sprigs fresh mint (optional)

1. Coat inside of **CROCK-POT**® slow cooker with nonstick cooking spray. Beat eggs, sugar and salt in large bowl with electric mixer at high speed until thick and pale yellow. Add flour; beat until smooth. Beat in evaporated milk and vanilla.

2. Pour batter into **CROCK-POT**® slow cooker. Place frozen cherries evenly over batter. Cover; cook on LOW 3½ to 4 hours or until flan is set. Serve warm with whipped cream, if desired. Garnish each serving with fresh cherry and mint.

Peach Cobbler

MAKES 4 TO 6 SERVINGS

2 packages (16 ounces *each*) frozen peaches, thawed and drained
½ cup plus 1 tablespoon sugar, divided
2 teaspoons ground cinnamon, divided

½ teaspoon ground nutmeg
¾ cup all-purpose flour
6 tablespoons butter, cubed
Whipped cream (optional)

1. Combine peaches, ½ cup sugar, 1½ teaspoons cinnamon and nutmeg in **CROCK-POT®** slow cooker; stir to blend.

2. Combine flour, remaining 1 tablespoon sugar and remaining ½ teaspoon cinnamon in small bowl. Cut in butter with pastry blender or two knives until mixture resembles coarse crumbs. Sprinkle over peach mixture. Cover; cook on HIGH 2 hours. Serve with whipped cream, if desired.

TIP: To make cleanup easier when cooking sticky or sugary foods, spray the inside of the **CROCK-POT®** slow cooker with nonstick cooking spray before adding ingredients.

Apple Crumble Pot

MAKES 6 TO 8 SERVINGS

4 Granny Smith apples (about 2 pounds *total*), cored and *each* cut into 8 wedges

1 cup packed dark brown sugar, divided

½ cup dried cranberries

1 cup plus 2 tablespoons biscuit baking mix, divided

2 tablespoons butter, cubed

1½ teaspoons ground cinnamon, plus additional for topping

1 teaspoon vanilla

¼ teaspoon ground allspice

½ cup rolled oats

3 tablespoons cold butter, cubed

½ cup chopped pecans

Whipped cream (optional)

1. Coat inside of **CROCK-POT**® slow cooker with nonstick cooking spray. Combine apples, ⅔ cup brown sugar, cranberries, 2 tablespoons baking mix, 2 tablespoons butter, 1½ teaspoons cinnamon, vanilla and allspice in **CROCK-POT**® slow cooker; toss gently to coat.

2. Combine remaining 1 cup baking mix, oats and remaining ⅓ cup brown sugar in large bowl. Cut in 3 tablespoons cold butter with pastry blender or two knives until mixture resembles coarse crumbs. Sprinkle evenly over filling in **CROCK-POT**® slow cooker. Top with pecans. Cover; cook on HIGH 2¼ hours or until apples are tender. *Do not overcook.*

3. Turn off heat. Let stand, uncovered, 15 to 30 minutes before serving. Top with whipped cream sprinkled with additional cinnamon, if desired.

Cherry Rice Pudding

MAKES 6 SERVINGS

1½ cups milk
1 cup hot cooked rice
3 eggs, beaten
½ cup sugar
¼ cup dried cherries or cranberries

½ teaspoon almond extract
¼ teaspoon salt
1 cup water
Ground nutmeg (optional)

1. Combine milk, rice, eggs, sugar, cherries, almond extract and salt in large bowl; stir to blend. Pour into greased 1½-quart casserole dish. Cover dish with buttered foil, butter side down.

2. Place rack in **CROCK-POT®** slow cooker; pour in water. Place casserole on rack. Cover; cook on LOW 4 to 5 hours.

3. Remove casserole from **CROCK-POT®** slow cooker. Let stand 15 minutes before serving. Garnish with nutmeg.

Spiced Vanilla Applesauce

MAKES 6 CUPS

---

5 pounds (about 10 medium) sweet apples (such as Fuji or Gala), peeled and cut into 1-inch pieces

½ cup water

2 teaspoons vanilla

1 teaspoon ground cinnamon

¼ teaspoon ground nutmeg

¼ teaspoon ground cloves

1. Combine apples, water, vanilla, cinnamon, nutmeg and cloves in **CROCK-POT®** slow cooker; stir to blend. Cover; cook on HIGH 3 to 4 hours or until apples are very tender.

2. Turn off heat. Mash mixture with potato masher to smooth out any large lumps. Let cool completely before serving.

Brioche and Amber Rum Custard

MAKES 4 TO 6 SERVINGS

2 tablespoons unsalted butter, melted

3½ cups whipping cream

4 eggs

½ cup packed dark brown sugar

⅓ cup amber or light rum

2 teaspoons vanilla

1 loaf (20 to 22 ounces) brioche bread, torn into pieces *or* 5 large brioche, cut into thirds*

½ cup coarsely chopped pecans

Caramel or butterscotch topping (optional)

If desired, trim and discard heels.

1. Coat inside of **CROCK-POT**® slow cooker with melted butter. Combine cream, eggs, brown sugar, rum and vanilla in large bowl; stir to blend.

2. Mound one fourth of brioche pieces in bottom of **CROCK-POT**® slow cooker. Ladle one fourth of cream mixture over brioche. Sprinkle with one third of pecans. Repeat layers with remaining brioche, cream mixture and pecans until all ingredients are used.

3. Cover; cook on LOW 3 to 3½ hours or on HIGH 1½ to 2 hours or until custard is set and toothpick inserted into center comes out clean.

4. Drizzle with caramel topping, if desired. Serve warm.

Fudge and Cream Pudding Cake

MAKES 8 TO 10 SERVINGS

2 tablespoons unsalted butter, melted
1 cup all-purpose flour
½ cup packed light brown sugar
5 tablespoons unsweetened cocoa powder, divided
2 teaspoons baking powder
½ teaspoon ground cinnamon

⅛ teaspoon salt
1 cup whipping cream
1 tablespoon vegetable oil
1 teaspoon vanilla
1½ cups hot water
½ cup packed dark brown sugar
Whipped cream (optional)

1. Prepare foil handles by tearing off three 18×2-inch strips heavy foil (or use regular foil folded to double thickness). Crisscross foil strips in spoke design; place in **CROCK-POT**® slow cooker. Coat inside of 5-quart **CROCK-POT**® slow cooker with butter.

2. Combine flour, light brown sugar, 3 tablespoons cocoa, baking powder, cinnamon and salt in medium bowl. Add cream, oil and vanilla; stir to blend. Pour batter into **CROCK-POT**® slow cooker.

3. Combine hot water, dark brown sugar and remaining 2 tablespoons cocoa in medium bowl; stir well. Pour sauce over cake batter. *Do not stir.* Cover; cook on HIGH 2 hours. Turn off heat. Let stand 10 minutes. Remove with foil handles to wire rack. Cut into wedges to serve. Serve with whipped cream, if desired.

Orange Soufflé

MAKES 10 SERVINGS

6 tablespoons unsalted butter, softened and divided
1¼ cups sugar, divided
Grated peel of 1 orange
½ cup milk
6 tablespoons all-purpose flour
8 egg yolks
6 tablespoons orange-flavored liqueur

1 tablespoon vanilla
10 egg whites
1 teaspoon salt
Whipped cream and fresh raspberries (optional)
Sprigs fresh mint (optional)

1. Coat inside of **CROCK-POT®** slow cooker with 2 tablespoons butter. Sprinkle ⅓ cup sugar evenly into bottom of **CROCK-POT®** slow cooker.

2. Place ⅔ cup sugar and orange peel in food processor or blender; process until orange peel is evenly ground and well combined.

3. Whisk orange sugar, milk and flour in medium saucepan; cook and stir over medium heat until just beginning to thicken. Bring to a boil over high heat; cook and stir 30 seconds. Remove from heat. Let mixture cool slightly; beat in egg yolks, one at a time. Add orange liqueur, remaining 4 tablespoons butter and vanilla to egg yolk mixture; let stand at room temperature 20 minutes to cool.

4. Beat egg whites in clean, dry bowl until foamy. Add salt; beat to soft peaks. Sprinkle in remaining ¼ cup sugar; beat to stiff peaks. Fold one quarter of beaten egg whites into cooled batter. Fold in remaining egg whites; gently remove to **CROCK-POT®** slow cooker. Cover; cook on HIGH 1 hour or until soufflé is fully set. Top with whipped cream and raspberries, if desired. Garnish with mint.

Bittersweet Chocolate-Espresso Crème Brûlée

MAKES 5 SERVINGS

½ cup chopped bittersweet chocolate
5 egg yolks
1½ cups whipping cream

½ cup granulated sugar
¼ cup espresso
¼ cup Demerara or raw sugar

1. Arrange five 6-ounce ramekins or custard cups inside of **CROCK-POT®** slow cooker. Pour enough water to come halfway up sides of ramekins (taking care to keep water out of ramekins). Divide chocolate among ramekins.

2. Whisk egg yolks in small bowl; set aside. Heat small saucepan over medium heat. Add cream, granulated sugar and espresso; cook and stir until mixture begins to boil. Pour hot cream in thin, steady stream into egg yolks, whisking constantly. Pour through fine mesh strainer into clean bowl.

3. Ladle into prepared ramekins over chocolate. Cover; cook on HIGH 1 to 2 hours or until custard is set around edges but still soft in centers. Carefully remove ramekins; cool to room temperature. Cover; refrigerate until serving.

4. Spread tops of custards with Demerara sugar just before serving. Serve immediately.

Fruit Ambrosia with Dumplings

MAKES 4 TO 6 SERVINGS

4 cups fresh or frozen fruit*

½ cup plus 2 tablespoons granulated sugar, divided

½ cup warm apple or cran-apple juice

2 tablespoons quick-cooking tapioca

1 cup all-purpose flour

1¼ teaspoons baking powder

¼ teaspoon salt

3 tablespoons butter or margarine, cubed

½ cup milk

1 egg

2 tablespoons packed light brown sugar, plus additional for garnish

Vanilla ice cream, whipped cream or fruity yogurt (optional)

*Use strawberries, raspberries or peaches.

1. Combine fruit, ½ cup granulated sugar, juice and tapioca in **CROCK-POT**® slow cooker. Cover; cook on LOW 5 to 6 hours or on HIGH 2½ to 3 hours.

2. Combine flour, remaining 2 tablespoons granulated sugar, baking powder and salt in medium bowl. Cut in butter using pastry blender or two knives until mixture resembles coarse crumbs. Whisk milk and egg in small bowl. Pour milk mixture into flour mixture. Stir until soft dough forms.

3. Drop dough by teaspoonfuls on top of fruit. Sprinkle with 2 tablespoons brown sugar. Cover; cook on HIGH 30 minutes to 1 hour or until toothpick inserted into centers of dumplings comes out clean.

4. Serve warm. Sprinkle dumplings with additional brown sugar, if desired. Top with ice cream, if desired.

Steamed Southern Sweet Potato Custard

MAKES 4 SERVINGS

---

1 can (16 ounces) cut sweet potatoes, drained

1 can (12 ounces) evaporated milk, divided

½ cup packed brown sugar

2 eggs, lightly beaten

1 teaspoon ground cinnamon

½ teaspoon ground ginger

¼ teaspoon salt

Whipped cream (optional)

Ground nutmeg (optional)

1. Place potatoes and ¼ cup evaporated milk in food processor or blender; process until smooth. Add remaining evaporated milk, brown sugar, eggs, cinnamon, ginger and salt; process until well blended. Pour into ungreased 1-quart soufflé dish. Cover tightly with foil. Crumple large sheet (15×12 inches) of foil; place in bottom of **CROCK-POT®** slow cooker. Pour 2 cups water over foil. Make foil handles. (See Note.)

2. Remove dish to **CROCK-POT®** slow cooker using foil handles. Cover; cook on HIGH 2½ to 3 hours or until toothpick inserted into center comes out clean.

3. Use foil strips to remove dish to wire rack. Uncover; let stand 30 minutes. Garnish with whipped cream and nutmeg.

> **NOTE:** To make foil handles, tear off three 18×2-inch strips of heavy-duty foil or use regular foil folded to double thickness. Crisscross strips in spoke design and place in **CROCK-POT®** slow cooker to make lifting dish easier.

Tequila-Poached Pears

MAKES 4 SERVINGS

4 Anjou pears, peeled
2 cups water
1 can (11½ ounces) pear nectar
1 cup tequila

½ cup sugar
Grated peel and juice of 1 lime
Vanilla ice cream (optional)

1. Place pears in **CROCK-POT**® slow cooker. Combine water, nectar, tequila, sugar, lime peel and lime juice in medium saucepan. Bring to a boil over medium-high heat, stirring frequently. Boil 1 minute; pour over pears.

2. Cover; cook on LOW 4 to 6 hours or on HIGH 2 to 3 hours or until pears are tender. Serve warm with poaching liquid and vanilla ice cream, if desired.

TIP: Poaching fruit in a sugar, juice or alcohol syrup helps the fruit retain its shape and become more flavorful.

Luscious Pecan Bread Pudding

MAKES 6 SERVINGS

3 cups day-old French bread cubes

3 tablespoons chopped pecans, toasted*

2¼ cups milk

2 eggs, beaten

½ cup plus 2 tablespoons sugar, divided

1 teaspoon vanilla

¾ teaspoon ground cinnamon, divided

¾ cup cranberry juice cocktail

1½ cups frozen pitted tart cherries

To toast pecans, spread in single layer in heavy skillet. Cook over medium heat 1 to 2 minutes or until nuts are lightly browned, stirring frequently.

1. Prepare foil handles. (See Note pg. 234) Toss bread cubes and pecans in soufflé dish that fits inside of **CROCK-POT®** slow cooker.

2. Combine milk, eggs, ½ cup sugar, vanilla and ½ teaspoon cinnamon in large bowl; pour over bread mixture in soufflé dish. Cover tightly with foil. Place soufflé dish in **CROCK-POT®** slow cooker. Pour hot water into **CROCK-POT®** slow cooker to about 1½ inches from top of soufflé dish. Cover; cook on LOW 2 to 3 hours.

3. Meanwhile, combine cranberry juice and remaining ¼ teaspoon cinnamon in small saucepan; stir in cherries. Bring to a boil over medium heat; cook 5 minutes. Remove from heat. Stir in remaining 2 tablespoons sugar.

4. Lift soufflé dish from **CROCK-POT®** slow cooker using foil handles. Serve bread pudding with cherry sauce.

Warm Peanut-Caramel Dip

MAKES 1¾ CUPS

¾ cup peanut butter
¾ cup caramel topping

⅓ cup milk
1 apple, thinly sliced

1. Combine peanut butter, caramel topping and milk in medium saucepan. Cook over medium heat until smooth and creamy, stirring occasionally.

2. Coat inside of **CROCK-POT**® "No Dial" slow cooker with nonstick cooking spray. Fill with warm dip. Serve with apples.

Pear Crunch

MAKES 4 SERVINGS

1 can (8 ounces) crushed pineapple in juice, undrained

¼ cup pineapple or apple juice

3 tablespoons dried cranberries

1½ teaspoons quick-cooking tapioca

¼ teaspoon vanilla

2 pears, cored and halved

¼ cup granola with almonds

1. Combine pineapple, pineapple juice, cranberries, tapioca and vanilla in **CROCK-POT®** slow cooker; stir to blend. Top with pears, cut sides down.

2. Cover; cook on LOW 3½ to 4½ hours. Arrange pear halves on serving plates. Spoon pineapple mixture over pear halves. Sprinkle with granola.

Figs Poached in Red Wine

MAKES 4 SERVINGS

2 cups dry red wine

1 cup packed brown sugar

12 dried Calimyrna or Mediterranean figs (about 6 ounces)

2 whole cinnamon sticks

1 teaspoon finely grated orange peel

4 tablespoons whipping cream (optional)

1. Combine wine, brown sugar, figs, cinnamon sticks and orange peel in **CROCK-POT®** slow cooker. Cover; cook on LOW 5 to 6 hours or on HIGH 4 to 5 hours.

2. Remove and discard cinnamon sticks. To serve, spoon syrup and cream, if desired, into serving dish. Top with figs.

Spicy Fruit Dessert

MAKES 4 TO 6 SERVINGS

2 cups canned pears, drained and diced

2 cups carambola (star fruit), sliced and seeds removed

1 can (6 ounces) frozen orange juice concentrate

¼ cup orange marmalade

¼ teaspoon pumpkin pie spice

Pound cake slices or ice cream

Whipped cream (optional)

Combine pears, carambola, orange juice concentrate, marmalade and pumpkin pie spice in **CROCK-POT®** slow cooker. Cover; cook on LOW 4 to 6 hours or on HIGH 2 to 3 hours or until cooked through. Serve warm over pound cake with whipped cream, if desired.

Metric Conversion Chart

VOLUME MEASUREMENTS (dry)

1/8 teaspoon = 0.5 mL
1/4 teaspoon = 1 mL
1/2 teaspoon = 2 mL
3/4 teaspoon = 4 mL
1 teaspoon = 5 mL
1 tablespoon = 15 mL
2 tablespoons = 30 mL
1/4 cup = 60 mL
1/3 cup = 75 mL
1/2 cup = 125 mL
2/3 cup = 150 mL
3/4 cup = 175 mL
1 cup = 250 mL
2 cups = 1 pint = 500 mL
3 cups = 750 mL
4 cups = 1 quart = 1 L

VOLUME MEASUREMENTS (fluid)

1 fluid ounce (2 tablespoons) = 30 mL
4 fluid ounces (1/2 cup) = 125 mL
8 fluid ounces (1 cup) = 250 mL
12 fluid ounces (1 1/2 cups) = 375 mL
16 fluid ounces (2 cups) = 500 mL

WEIGHTS (mass)

1/2 ounce = 15 g
1 ounce = 30 g
3 ounces = 90 g
4 ounces = 120 g
8 ounces = 225 g
10 ounces = 285 g
12 ounces = 360 g
16 ounces = 1 pound = 450 g

DIMENSIONS

1/16 inch = 2 mm
1/8 inch = 3 mm
1/4 inch = 6 mm
1/2 inch = 1.5 cm
3/4 inch = 2 cm
1 inch = 2.5 cm

OVEN TEMPERATURES

250°F = 120°C
275°F = 140°C
300°F = 150°C
325°F = 160°C
350°F = 180°C
375°F = 190°C
400°F = 200°C
425°F = 220°C
450°F = 230°C

BAKING PAN SIZES

Utensil	Size in Inches/Quarts	Metric Volume	Size in Centimeters
Baking or Cake Pan (square or rectangular)	8×8×2	2 L	20×20×5
	9×9×2	2.5 L	23×23×5
	12×8×2	3 L	30×20×5
	13×9×2	3.5 L	33×23×5
Loaf Pan	8×4×3	1.5 L	20×10×7
	9×5×3	2 L	23×13×7
Round Layer Cake Pan	8×1½	1.2 L	20×4
	9×1½	1.5 L	23×4
Pie Plate	8×1¼	750 mL	20×3
	9×1¼	1 L	23×3
Baking Dish or Casserole	1 quart	1 L	—
	1½ quart	1.5 L	—
	2 quart	2 L	—